21 DAY LOAN ITEM

ALECK .

In 2003, Alecky
production, *Come*
London, and later transi.
Out Award for Best Performa.
went on to make *All the Right People Co...*
Wimbledon Theatre). Alecky has since created ...
Fields (The Courtyard, Hereford); *Cruising* (Bush Theatre, London); *The Girlfriend Experience* (Royal Court Theatre and Young Vic, London); *I Only Came Here for Six Months* (KVS and Les Halles, Brussels); and *Do We Look Like Refugees?!*, a joint project for the National Theatre Studio and the Rustaveli Theatre, Georgia (Assembly Rooms, Edinburgh Festival Fringe, 2010; winner of Fringe First Award). For television she has written *A Man in a Box* (IWC and Channel 4).

D0514252

ADAM CORK

Adam Cork's theatre work includes scores and sound designs for *Danton's Death, Phèdre, All's Well That Ends Well* and *Time and the Conways* at the National; *ENRON* at Chichester Festival Theatre, Royal Court, West End and Broadway; *Romeo and Juliet* and *The Tempest* for the RSC; *King Lear, Red* (also Broadway), *A Streetcar Named Desire, Othello, The Chalk Garden, Creditors, The Wild Duck, John Gabriel Borkman* and *Caligula* at the Donmar Warehouse; *Hamlet* (also Broadway), *Ivanov* and *Madame de Sade* for the Donmar at Wyndham's; *King Lear* at Liverpool Everyman and Young Vic; *No Man's Land* and *A View from the Bridge* at the Duke of York's; *Six Characters in Search of an Author* at the Gielgud and Chichester; *Don Carlos* at Gielgud and Sheffield; *The Glass Menagerie* at the Apollo; *The Last Days of Judas Iscariot* and *The Late Henry Moss* at the Almeida; *Faustus* and *Paradise Lost* for Headlong; and *The Cherry Orchard* at Sheffield Crucible. In 2011 he won the Olivier Award for Best Sound Design for *King Lear*. In 2010 he won the Tony Award for Best Sound Design of a Play for *Red*, and was nominated for Best Original Score and Best Sound Design for *ENRON*. He was previously nominated for the Best Sound Design of a Play Tony for *Macbeth* (2008). He was nominated for an Olivier Award for Best Sound Design for *Suddenly Last Summer* (2005); as well as for four Drama Desk Awards: Outstanding Music in a Play for *Frost/Nixon* (2007) and *Red* (2010), and Outstanding Sound Design for *Macbeth* (2008) and *ENRON* (2010). Film and TV includes *Frances Tuesday, Macbeth, Re-ignited, Imprints, Bust* and *Tripletake*. Radio includes *Losing Rosalind, The Luneberg Variation, The Chalk Garden, The Colonel-Bird, Don Carlos, Othello* and *On the Ceiling*.

LONDON ROAD

Book and Lyrics by
Alecky Blythe

Music and Lyrics by
Adam Cork

NICK HERN BOOKS
London
www.nickhernbooks.co.uk

A Nick Hern Book

London Road first published in Great Britain as a paperback original in 2011 by Nick Hern Books Limited, The Glasshouse, 49a Goldhawk Road, London W12 8QP

Reprinted 2011, 2012 (twice)

London Road copyright © 2011 Alecky Blythe and Adam Cork

Alecky Blythe and Adam Cork have asserted their right to be identified as the authors of this work

Cover image of aerial view of Ipswich, UK, by **getmapping**®
Cover design by Ned Hoste, 2H

Typeset by Nick Hern Books, London
Printed in the UK by Mimeo Ltd, Huntingdon, Cambridgeshire PE29 6XX

A CIP catalogue record for this book is available from the British Library

ISBN   978 1 84842 176 9

Singing for Real

Development of the project

In the spring of 2007 I was invited to take part in the writers and composers week at the National Theatre Studio. The purpose of the week was to pair up a handful of writers and composers, put the pairings in a room together and see if any interesting discoveries were made by the end of it. The wonderful thing about the Studio is that on the surface it gives artists the opportunity to experiment and 'get things wrong'. However, underneath this relaxed, cosy veneer, those who are lucky enough to workshop projects there know that in some cases there is the slim but real potential for them to be brought to life on the South Bank. So it was in an atmosphere of latent dreams that Adam and I first met.

I was delighted to be at the workshop, as working with music was a voyage into uncharted territory for me. As my work is made from recorded everyday conversations and replicated by actors as authentically as possible, musical theatre, with its necessary affectation, is not a genre that sits easily with me. I wanted to find out if I could adapt the verbatim technique in a way which incorporated music without losing its honesty.

Development of the technique

I work using a technique originally created by Anna Deavere Smith. Deavere Smith was the first to combine the journalistic technique of interviewing her subjects with the art of reproducing their words accurately in performance. It was passed on to me via Mark Wing-Davey in his workshop 'Drama Without Paper'.

The technique involves going into a community of some sort and recording conversations with people, which are then edited to become the script of the play. However, the actors do not see the text. The edited recordings are played live to the actors through earphones during the rehearsal process, and onstage in performance. The actors listen to the audio and repeat what they hear. They copy not just the words but exactly the way in which they were first spoken. Every cough, stutter and hesitation is reproduced. Up till now for my previous shows, the actors have not learnt the lines at any point. By listening to the audio during performances the actors are helped to remain accurate to the original recordings, rather than slipping into their own patterns of speech or embellishment.

The considerable musical dimension of *London Road* has required a rethinking of the presentation of this recorded-delivery verbatim technique. By setting some of the material to music – even though Adam has been scrupulous in notating the tune of the spoken voice so that it remains faithful to how it was first said – the fact that at times characters sing their words instead of speak them as they did in real life, is a departure from the purer verbatim form of my past endeavours. In keeping with the songs being learnt from the score, the spoken text has also been learnt. With both the songs and the spoken text the audio has remained intrinsic to the process, so that the original delivery as well as the words are learnt.

I had arrived at the writers and composers week armed with a range of material with which we could experiment – but it was the interviews that I recorded in the winter of 2006 in Ipswich that best lent themselves to musical intervention. What Adam and I discovered with the music was that it succeeded in binding together shared sentiments that were being echoed throughout the town during those worrying times. More importantly, Adam was able to set these words to music by following the cadence and rhythms of the original speech patterns so accurately that it did not diminish their verisimilitude. I was also excited to have a new tool at my disposal with the songwriting. By creating verses and choruses, I could shape the material for narrative and dramatic effect further than I had ever been able to do before. To my surprise, we had between us the seeds of both the subject and the technique to take to another stage.

Development of the story

My first interviews from Ipswich were collected on 15th December 2006; five bodies had been found but no arrests had been made. The town was at the height of its fear. I had been gripped and appalled by the spiralling tragedies that were unravelling in Ipswich during that dark time. It would of course be a shocking experience for any community, but the fact that it took place in this otherwise peaceful rural town, never before associated with high levels of crime or soliciting, made it all the more upsetting for the people who lived there. It was not what was mainly being reported in the media about the victims or the possible suspects that drew me to Ipswich, but the ripples it created in the wider community in the lives of those on the periphery. Events of this proportion take hold in all sorts of areas outside the lead story, and that is what I wanted to explore.

It was not until six months later, when I returned to Ipswich to gauge the temperature of the town after the arrests but before the trial, that I stumbled upon what was to me the most interesting development so far. A Neighbourhood Watch that had been set up at the time of the murders had organised a 'London Road in Bloom' competition and the street could not have looked more different from when it had been besieged by the media the winter before. Hanging baskets lined the roads and front gardens were bursting with floral displays. Such was the impact of the terrible happenings in that area that the community had come together and set up a series of events, from gardening competitions to quiz nights, in order to try to heal itself. Although this had some coverage in the local press, the national media had not reported this final and important chapter of the story. Over the course of the next two years, I regularly revisited the residents of London Road to chart their full recovery.

I would like to say a special thank you to everyone who shared their stories with me, particularly the members of the London Road Neighbourhood Watch, without whose generosity the play would not have been possible.

Alecky Blythe, 2011

Saying in Tune

When I first met Alecky at the National Theatre Studio almost four years ago, as part of an experimental week which brought together composers and playwrights, I had no idea that I'd be working with a 'verbatim' practitioner. And when Alecky explained the concept and methods of this documentary form to me, I have to admit my very first thought was 'How on earth can I turn this into music?' But when we started listening to her interviews, I began to feel that this could be an inspiring new approach to songwriting, or, more accurately, an exciting development of an existing way of composing songs. Whenever I've set conventional texts to music, I've always spoken the words to myself, and transcribed the rhythms and the melodic rise and fall of my own voice, to try and arrive at the most truthful and direct expression of the text. And here was an opportunity to refine that to a much purer process, without any authorial or poetic interpretation (not to mention my own bad acting) polluting the connection between the actual subject and his or her representation in music.

And so we began, with a few ideas about what we wanted the piece to be. My initial aim was that the music should be as articulated as possible, otherwise we wouldn't be doing justice to the reality and the uniqueness of the depicted people. I also wanted to seize the challenge of taking an experimental idea and developing it into something which could be interesting as both music and drama. I didn't want to reference any overall musical style, but rather, discover responses suggested by the material on a moment-by-moment basis. For that reason I didn't foresee much cross-pollination of musical motifs from one song to another, although I did want the identity of each individual song to be clear; I felt this was the only way I could create musical meaning from this un-versified, spontaneously spoken text. I also hoped that, in the spirit of the documentary concept, the musical score would be like a time capsule inside which the speech rhythms would be captured and contained, frozen and fossilised in music just as they have a fixed existence on Alecky's recordings. And I wanted to find a way of singing with the quality of speech, which is altogether different from either an operatic or a conventional musical-theatre vocal style. In this last wish I have been very lucky, as our Musical Director David Shrubsole and the voice expert Mary Hammond have together helped the cast develop and maintain a speech-like way of singing which engages their prodigious techniques from a variety of disciplines.

At the outset I imagined that the process of finding a way to set words to music while staying faithful to the ideals of verbatim documentary theatre would eventually lead us to a whole new set of ideal principles, a properly developed written recipe for how we should conduct this experiment. In the event, we never did arrive at anything that prescriptive. In fact, as you experience the production you're presented with the evolution of our approach. Some of the songs and fragments written towards the beginning of our process of development – early works that have 'made the cut' – are quite different from the more recent pieces. As I transcribed and composed and thought about it all, I found myself getting better and quicker at doing it, and representing the music of the speech rhythms with increasing forensic zeal, to the point where transcriptions from earlier in the process started to feel a little naïve, or less faithful to the documentary ideal than the later songs. But the slightly freer hand I gave myself initially had produced some interesting results, and abandoning the earlier music seemed to diminish the experience somehow.

Having said that, it's very easy retrospectively to describe what we've done in terms of 'rules', or at least to say that there are some things that generally seem to happen. The lack of rhyme or consistent meter or line length in spontaneous speech, even after we've structured the recordings into 'verses' and 'choruses', results in labyrinthine tunes which offer hardly any repetitive potential in themselves, as rhythmic or melodic material. So our instinct has been for the most part to contain these anarchic lines within fairly solid musical structures, and these containers are often built out of key elements of the transcribed voice, translated into harmonic progressions, or rhythms in the accompaniment. And on the occasions when this approach has repeatedly led towards the wrong sort of song, I've had a good long think about what the song should express musically and composed a 'container' unconnected with the musical surface of the words, but inspired by their literal content, or the tone in which they are spoken, or the mood of the situation in which they were uttered, or that of the situation which they describe.

It's also possible to notice some effects of the verbatim song forms we've developed, whilst confessing that many of them were unforeseen! A presentational style seems to suit the material better than a psychological one. As with non-musical documentary theatre, the actors find they are inhabited (or possessed) by the voices of the people they represent, rather than creating roles using the traditional rules of characterisation. I find that hearing the natural speech patterns sung in this way can have the effect of distancing the audience from the 'character', and even the 'story', but in a positive way that alters the quality of listening. Making spontaneously spoken words formal, through musical accompaniment and repetition, has the potential to explode the thought of a moment into slow motion, and can allow us more deeply to contemplate what's being expressed. This seems particularly interesting when many different people speak about the same thought or feeling.

In fact, the choral presentation of this story in particular seems to underline the ritual aspect of human communal experience. The experiences captured on this stage are not new to our species, whether it's the healing process after a tragedy, the gathering of forces within a community to find and punish a dangerous individual, or the telling of all these events to the wider community. This is deeply ancient, shared human experience in all its facets, no matter how much professionalism and the division of labour distance us from each other today. The people of Ipswich, the residents of London Road, and the news media, play their part in this ritual, and so do we, in presenting this piece of choric theatre.

Adam Cork, 2011

London Road was first performed in the Cottesloe auditorium of the National Theatre, London, on 14 April 2011 (previews from 7 April), with the following cast (only main roles are indicated):

CLARE BURT	*Jan*
ROSALIE CRAIG	*Helen*
KATE FLEETWOOD	*Julie*
HAL FOWLER	*Tim*
NICK HOLDER	*Ron*
CLAIRE MOORE	*June*
MICHAEL SHAEFFER	*Alfie*
NICOLA SLOANE	*Rosemary*
PAUL THORNLEY	*Dodge*
HOWARD WARD	*Terry*
DUNCAN WISBEY	*Gordon*

MUSICIANS

MARTIN BRIGGS	*Percussion*
JON GINGELL	*Guitar / Bass Guitar*
RACHEL ELLIOTT	*Woodwind*
CHRISTIAN FORSHAW	*Woodwind*
SIMON HARAM	*Woodwind*
IAN TOWNSEND	*Keyboards*

Director	Rufus Norris
Designer	Katrina Lindsay
Lighting Designer	Bruno Poet
Movement Director	Javier De Frutos
Sound Designer	Paul Arditti
Music Director	David Shrubsole
Associate Music Director	Ian Townsend

The production transferred to the Olivier auditorium of the National Theatre on 28 July 2012, with the following changes to the cast and creative team:

JAMES DOHERTY	*Terry*
LINZI HATELEY	*Helen*
STEVE SMITH	*Guitar / Bass Guitar*

LONDON ROAD

Characters

RON
JULIE
GORDON
HELEN
ROSEMARY
TERRY
JUNE
JAN
ALFIE
DODGE
ORANGE GIRL
RADIO TECHIE
RADIO DJ
STEPHANIE
KIRSTY
KIRSTY'S BOYFRIEND
MARKET STALL HOLDER 1
MARKET STALL HOLDER 2
MARKET STALL HOLDER 3
LEAFLET GIRL 1
LEAFLET GIRL 2
TIM
STARBUCKS GIRL 1
STARBUCKS GIRL 2
STELLA
OLD LADY
CAROL 'CREAMS'
HECTOR
MARK
WAYNE
GRAHAME
YOKEL
GRAHAME COOPER
MARK

WAYNE
ITN CAMERAMAN
JASON
LIDL MAN
LIDL WOMAN
HARRY
POLICEMAN
BBC NEWSREADER
CHRIS EAKIN
WOMAN 1
WOMAN 2
MAN
PRODUCER 1
FEMALE REPORTER
MALE REPORTER 1
SIMON NEWTON
SEB
ANGLIA NEWSREADER
REBECCA
SARAH
NICOLA
KELLY McCORMACK
PRODUCER 2
MALE REPORTER 2
CAMERAMAN
FIVE NEWSREADER
MARY NIGHTINGALE
WARD COUNCILLOR
    CAROL
INGA
ALAN
CHRIS
JEAN

The Residents of London Road

Ron and Rosemary   Ron is the chairman of the Neighbourhood Watch. He and his wife Rosemary moved to London Road ten years ago from Peckham for their retirement.

Julie   Julie is the Neighbourhood Watch Events Organiser. She is a keen gardener and came up with the idea for 'London Road in Bloom'. Originally from rural Essex, she has been a London Road resident for twenty years.

Helen and Gordon   Helen is the Secretary of the Neighbourhood Watch. She and her husband Gordon are both retired teachers. Gordon plays lead guitar in The Git Band, who regularly play at Neighbourhood Watch social gatherings.

Jan and Tim   Jan and Tim are on the Neighbourhood Watch committee. Jan is a part-time carer for the elderly and has been living in London Road for twenty-six years.

Dodge   Dodge is a committee member and every year hosts the 'London Road in Bloom' barbecue in his back garden. A window cleaner by trade, he has possibly been living in the street for longer than anyone.

Terry and June   Terry and June met each other late in life. June worked for years at the John Player Cigarette factory in Ipswich. Terry was a building site plant operator until being made redundant. They are both keen line-dancers.

Alfie   London Road was Alfie's home for twenty years until a recent move. For three years in succession he was the winner of the Best Overall Garden in the 'London Road in Bloom' competition.

Note on the Text

Songs and sung text are indicated with italics.

Emphasis and stress are indicated with bold.

A forward slash in the text (/) indicates the point at which the next speaker interrupts.

Inconsistences in spelling and grammar are deliberate and indicate idiosyncracies in the speech and delivery of the characters.

Setting

London Road and various other locations in Ipswich. December 2006 to July 2008.

This text went to press before the end of rehearsals and so may differ slightly from the play as performed.

ACT ONE

Section One

Church hall just off London Road.

The original audio recording of RON*'s opening speech is heard over the PA in the auditorium. It fades out as* RON *starts to sing.*

Song – 'Neighbourhood Watch AGM'

RON. *Good evening. (Beat.) Welcome. (Beat.) This really is our first AGM after we reconstituted in 2006 and then all the awful events happened and we became stronger an' stronger. Erm (Beat.) aft' so after our er reconstitution we made a lot – we made a lot of progress in regenerating this street. We've put new signs up, thanks to Ken. Hope-hopefully the problem with the girls has disappeared. We don't see them now. I believe there are still a few round in Hanford Road but er (Beat.) we really can't concern ourselves with them. The street has got much better in the last year. I think the police have done exceptionally well under exceptional circumstances to clear the streets as they have done. Our problem now is to keep them up so they may have commit them to Lo' – ya know – this is gonna continue. That they are still gonna help the girls who need helpin' or-or jump on the ones who don't. Our problem is to keep the police to that commitment. The Chief Constable said to us in the police briefing that this is gonna go on for five years. We gotta keep them to it! We can't let other priorities take – take over otherwise we're just gonna slip back. I wanna say 'thank you' to the police. Thank them becos representatives here and the Ward Councillors, the County Councillors who have done a lot to help us. An' so 'thank you very much all of you'. Yeah forthcoming events, Julie.*

JULIE. *Very similar to last year really. We're still gonna carry on the quiz night. Fish 'n' chip shupper yet again. So ya know more the merrier, friends, family. We always get a good number anyway and we have a cracking night so hopefully see you all there with yer friends and family. An' also our 'London Road in Bloom' contest again. Such a success last time. I was really, really pleased. It's a lot of hard work but beautiful gardens. Ya know everybody enjoyed themselves. So get thinkin' about yerr gardens, yer designs, hangin' baskets an' so forth so I'd like to see as many as possible.* (*Beat.*) That's about it.

RON. That's it. Thank you.

Beat.

JULIE. It's – we thought well with everything happening over the Christmas period with the prostitutes goin' missin' an – and being murdered an' so forth – we needed to get together as a community. We got a lot of bad press erm when it was all goin' on sayin' sort 'Lon – London Road was a prostutute area' an' so forth like that and we jus' got absolutely cheesed off with it as a – as a community it **is** – it's **not** nice bein' labelled. So we'd got together an' got a Neighbourhood Watch up an' runnin' an' we've managed to get a real good committee goin'.

GORDON. But I think (*Beat.*) ya'ow, the murders have **brought** the community together / and made (*Beat.*) –

HELEN. / Mm.

GORDON. – restarted the neighbourhood – much (*Beat.*) more of a priority for more people.

HELEN. It's probably given us a common – a really / common cause.

GORDON. / Mmmm.

RON. Yeah Helen is the secretary of the / (*Beat.*) Neighbourhood Watch committee. I'm the chairman (*Beat.*) it – we were over**whelmed** with (*Beat.*) people comin' wantin' ta join (*Beat.*) because a the (*Beat.*) **murders**. An'

then of course the err (*Pause.*) Julie is a (*Beat.*) **keen**
gardener – you've – seen her window boxes obvisly.
(*Pause.*) **She** suggested this at one of the big meetings – an'
she said 'Let's 'ave a "London Road in Bloom" competition'
(*Beat.*) and we all said 'Yeah, that'll be nice.'

ROSEMARY. / Neighbourhood Watch.

JULIE. I come up with the idea of doin' 'London Road in
Bloom' (*Beat.*) to make the area look pretty – an' that an'
getting people – involved – an' getting interested in their road
and their homes again. You know – it's people 'ave put –
hangin' baskets out **this** year, that (*Beat.*) have never done –
hangin' baskets and pots before in their lives. (*Pause.*) But
they made an effort (*Beat.*) for the 'London Road in Bloom'.
Come in my garden, cos I'll er – come in my back garden cos
Bailey will jus' bark otherwise. We can talk a bit better there.

Underscored:

JUNE. I don't know a weed from a plant I don't. But I did do
a-a pot.

TERRY. Yes we got er June's pot. / An' these are double
petunias.

JUNE. / My pot. What are they?

JAN. My – well my daughter bought that down for me. I've
never done baskets before so that was nice to… yes.

JULIE. And th' Mayor came out in the morning at ten o'clock
(*Beat.*) and came u – walked up and down the road with us,
and picked some winners.

Pause.

GORDON. We wouldn't have got that without the murders
would we? The fact the Lord **Mayor** (*Beat.*) is it the Lord
Mayor? / Well the Mayor – anyway (*Beat.*) –

HELEN. / No.

GORDON. – fact the **Mayor** turned out to judge our
competition. Ha.

HELEN. Yeah.

RON. The Mayor ya wanderin' round with 'er chain on walking up and down – I's (*laughing*) **frightened** to death she was walkin' up an' down withachain (*Beat.*) thought 'somebody's gonna be pinchin' this thing'! (*Pause.*) And I thought, 'yeah – **tak**in' a risk'. (*Pause.*) Ah-our reputation round / 'ere –

ROSEMARY. / Well, she obviously felt safe in London Road. Oh we didn't win any prizes.

HELEN. We won a prize didn't we?

GORDON. Yep. / Commented on our neat lawn didn't they?

HELEN. / Yeaah so –

HELEN. Oh they yeah – commented on our lovely lawn.

ALFIE. I won the first prize. So – it'll be in the papers on Thursday. Yes. Well I had people coming all week here ya know what I mean – everybody. Like Sunday – some people they come from holiday – tourists – they come down 'ere. (*Beat.*) Chinese they got – I said 'Come in.' An' she stood there an' he took a photos over there. (*Beat.*) Tourists. Something's come out of per day. Today the er st-*Evening Star*'s come down and yerself – who's gonna be next? Ha ha.

RON. The more publicity we get – around here – the less likely it is – I think – fer de (*Beat.*) ne'er-do-wells ta start creepin' back. (*Beat.*) Get the – uh (*Pause.*) I mustn't keep sayin' this I keep tellin' (*Beat.*) every meetin' we hold 'we gotta get this street tarted **up**'. (*Laughs heartily.*) An' they always say 'it's not the right choice a words'. Yeah.

JULIE. If you make yer house look nice (*Beat.*) and feel good about where you're living – then you'll enjoy – you'll enjoy life a hell of a lot bedda. When you're waterin' em people come and say how nice it looks (*Beat.*) and that makes you feel proud to be where you are. (*Beat.*) Very pleased with it. Yeah, it's gardens galore, ha ha.

Song – 'London Road in Bloom'

JULIE. *I got nearly seventeen hangin' baskets in this back garden – believe it or not. Begonias, petunias an – erm – impatiens an' things.*

ALFIE. *Marigolds, petunias. We got up there, we got busy Lizzies, hangin' geraniums alright – / see the hangin' lobelias, petunias in the basket – hangin' basket. That's a fuchsia.*

DODGE. / *There's all sorts in that basket anyway.*

JAN. *Err there is a special name I just call them lilies. They're a lily type. There is a special name. An' for the first time this year I've got a couple of erm – baskets.*

TERRY. *Hangin' baskets, variegated ivy in there which makes a nice show. Then you've got err these sky-blue whatever they are ve – ver – ber la la. That's err little purple ones.*

HELEN. *Rhubarb, the old-fashioned margarites, the daisies.*

GORDON. *The roses have done really well this year.*

HELEN. *Gave an extra point for havin' basil on the windowsill didn't she. / Ha ha ha.*

GORDON. / *Yeah.*

Section Two

London Road sitting rooms.

DODGE. Yer**self** – I mean – you'd be – as far as I'm – as-as (*Beat.*) like, as far as I'm aware – about the only person that **has** – actually come down here, and **asked** the residents how they feel. There's been lots of berm – lots about the girls – ya know-all their problems and erm. And I find it astounding that – yeah, okay, there were five (*Beat.*) distinct victims there – but there's also **other** victims, you know the people that lived here and had ta (*Beat.*) put up with it.

JULIE. It was – It was absolutely awful. Cos of the children. I've got – I've got teenage girls. I've got a twenty-year-old and a seventeen-year-old and I've got a fourteen-year-old boy. So yeah they were havin' to erm (*Beat.*) make sure they got their mobile phones on them. Erm. My middle daughter works at Next and Next were very good erm they weren't allowing any of their work staff leaving the **store** (*Beat.*) un-less there was an adult there to pick them up. They weren't letting them leave them. If they couldn't have find anyone to bring 'em home, they'd book them a taxi t' bring them back home. So yeah it was all – it was all of that worry.

JUNE. When they found the (*Beat.*) no, first of all the gir – we'll say, one girl was missun (*Beat.*) never dreamt, then, did we, / really (*Beat.*) what was hapnin – just **one** girl –

TERRY. / No (*Beat.*) we jus' –

JUNE. – go missun. (*Beat.*) Like, we'll say (*Beat.*) a week later, they find a body (*Pause.*) no – no arrests, or anyfing, they found a body (*Beat.*) an' then you find in the paper (*Beat.*) or radio telly – a**nother** girl is missun (*Beat.*) from **Ipswich** – an' they find a**nother** body – an' this I mean – imagine, this went on fer **five times** (*Beat.*) till they found **five** bodies (*Beat.*) an' **all** prostitutes.

JULIE. There was a **lot** of fear from a **lot** of people. I think it's the biggest thing that's ever-ever happened in Ipswich. Ya ·know everything else was put on the back-burner. It was – the main topic of conversation was (*Beat.*) was the **girls**.

Marketplace.

Song – 'Everyone is Very Very Nervous'

ALL. *Everyone is very very nervous*
And very unsure of everything basically.

ORANGE GIRL. *I'm a bit of an actress so I can tell –*
You can ask me anything

Er her her her
It's erm definitely changed the mood
It's quite. Yeah. S'quite an unpleasant feeling
because you're
constantly I find that I'm walking through thinking
'Well is it him, is it him?'
Yah I think it's uhm
put th'
Ipswich on the map for the wrong reasons unfortunately.

RADIO TECHIE. *We're not actually sellin', it's actually free.*
Just free personal safety alarms on behalf of Town 102.
Local radio station in Ipswich.
Er just handing away free personal alarms
because of what's – in the wake of what's
been happening in Ipswich recently.

ALL. *Everyone is very very nervous erm*
And very unsure of everything basically.

RADIO TECHIE. *And I mean these are just flying out basic –*
we've only been out here about half an hour
and we've nearly run out of stock
so yeah yeah definitely.
I mean the best person to talk to is the bloke
by the gen – by the erm lamp-post over there
cos he's the actual DJ, I'm just promotions.

RADIO DJ. *Obviously you gotta lotta people goin' out f' th'*
     weekend
th' gonna be a bit worried
So erm we're handing out personal alarms to erm
a t' sort of ladies out shopping today
So that, so that's why we're here.

ALL. *Everyone's very very nervous*
Obviously you gotta lotta people goin' out f' th' weekend
th' gonna be a bit worried
So erm we're handing out personal alarms to erm
a t' sort of ladies out shopping today
So that, so that's why we're here.

Repeat x 2.

Underscored:

STEPHANIE. I dunno – i, it **is** kind of a dodgy feeling cuz like no one stays out at night, now (*Beat.*) but – I like stayin' out a night, so if I walk around it's like, '**Why's** there no one out?' (*Beat.*) But – ye know. (*Pause.*) Cuz I fink, if yer gonna die, yer – gonna die – so… (*Beat, laughs.*) Thass that'ss **my** – point of view. (*Beat.*) Yeah. (*Beat.*) Are you quite conscious of the murders which happened round here? (*Pause.*) He doesn't care you see, that's the attitude of people. They just don't care. The news and the press just hype it all up ya know. Cos it's Suffolk, nothing ever happens in Suffolk. If it happened in London no one would care. Cos everyone gets stabbed in London every day. Isn't that right? Alec come an' talk. (*Pause.*) He's running away. Do you wanna go round here? Sounds like a fight.

ALEC. Oi! Ashley – Nav! Oi!

Shouting and yelling in the background.

STEPHANIE. Ya see. Stuff always happens. It's a load of bollocks but… we like it. You alright Kirsty?

KIRSTY. The stupid thing is I used to walk home at five o'clock in the morning on my own. I'm not doin' that any more – not on my own. But yeah I used to walk home sessed on my own all the time. I actually took taxi money out with me Monday which I never do. I'd spent the taxi on drink huh, but I didn't – I kept it separate. I had the taxi money. / It was separate the whole night.

KIRSTY'S BOYFRIEND. / That's my girlfriend do ya know what I mean, if anything happened to 'er I'd fuckin' fuck – kill everyone. Love the girl don't I? / I'm not gonna fuckin' hurt – hurt her am I?

KIRSTY. / Huh.

KIRSTY'S BOYFRIEND. Nothin's gonna happen to her. Just worry too much. (*Kisses her.*) Becos at the end of the day she

can look after herself anywhere, yeah? But when she's got a
person which is a legend anyway and an ex – boxer / there's
a lot of difference int there? Yeah? Simple as that. It's the
truth man.

/ KIRSTY *laughs*.

Song – 'Everyone is Very Very Nervous' (continued)

RADIO DJ. *Obviously you gotta lotta people goin' out f' th'*
     weekend
th' gonna be a bit worried
So erm we're handing out personal alarms to erm
a t' sort of ladies out shopping today
So that, so that's why we're here.

ALL. *Obviously you gotta lotta people goin' out f' th' weekend*
th' gonna be a bit worried
So erm we're handing out personal alarms to erm
a t' sort of ladies out shopping today
So that, so that's why we're here.

Underscored:

MUM IN QUEUE. Can I have one for mi daughter please? /
Thank you.

RADIO DJ. / Certainly. S'course you can. Would you like one
of those?

ORANGE GIRL. Problemis we nee – we're tryin' a buy some
because we need seven for our store?

RADIO DJ. Okay well we can sort / that out for you.

ORANGE GIRL. / Is that possible. Do you mind?

RADIO DJ. Yeah I should think we can do that. Hang on. One,
two…

ORANGE GIRL. Cuz it's very odd. It's very surreal I think,
personally.

RADIO DJ. Yeah oh definitely yeah.

ORANGE GIRL. Knowing that erm. Ya know a friend of mine was in New Zealand at the time when this was all going, she's jus' come back an' she heard about it over there – / is quite 'cuse the pun but 'alarming'. / So ha ha. It's kind of you know. It's – I think that's probably… So. But I'm gonna – i – gonna steal all of 'is alarms now / look. Thank you very very much.

RADIO DJ. / Mmm.

RADIO DJ. / Ha ha ha.

RADIO DJ. / No no.

RADIO DJ. Okay no worries.

ORANGE GIRL. Cheers bye.

MARKET STALL HOLDER 1. That's like Deben- / hams.

MARKET STALL HOLDER 2. / Debenhams they're layin' on minibuses for the – all the lady staff an' that to get 'ome at night-time just in case.

MARKET STALL HOLDER 3. Taxis an' things.

MARKET STALL HOLDER 2. Taxis yeah.

MARKET STALL HOLDER 1. All stores. An' Willis as well weren' it?

MARKET STALL HOLDER 2. Yeah.

MARKET STALL HOLDER 3. An' Marks an' Spencers are doin' the same.

LEAFLET GIRL 1. Erm we've jus' got leaflets off the police an' we're handin' 'em out.

LEAFLET GIRL 2. Yeah for the safety of young people and old people. It's like a text-message service.

LEAFLET GIRL 1. You send a text to this service. If you don't cancel it by eleven o'clock it will send a text message to your closest contact. If they can't reach hold of you they will call the police.

ALL. *Obviously you gotta lotta people goin' out f' th' weekend*
th' gonna be a bit worried
So erm we're handing out personal alarms to erm
a t' sort of ladies out shopping today
So that, so that's why we're here.
Everyone is very very nervous.

Repeat x 2.

London Road sitting rooms.

GORDON. The police kept issuin' all these strange – things
about what you should an' shouldn't do, but they **never** said
'don't be a prostitute an' don't get into a **stranger's car'**
which is / (*Pause, laughs.*) which was the obvious thing
really wasn't it, / because everybody else / was quite safe
walkin' the streets.

HELEN. / Yeah.

HELEN. / Mmm.

HELEN. / Mmm.

HELEN. Yeah. Well we assumed. We assumed. Particularly
when – / I mean it was just prostitutes he seemed to be
(*Beat.*) murdering. (*Gently laughs.*)

GORDON. / We assumed.

DODGE. I just think like ya know that okay. The erm – the
people that lived round here wer-were just a bit more vigilant
like ya know – they go out in couples ya know and then so I
don't think there was the fear – that – ya know. It's weird
that I don't think that we – were going to be attacked.

ROSEMARY. No no – cos I think at my age erm, I could see
that what he was targeting – sort of, slightly younger than
me. Yeah – no I wasn't frightened at all.

RON. I can't say that people were concerned. The
Neighbourhood Watch people – the main concern was once
again – callin' us a red-light area.

JUNE. Because he hant been caught (*Beat*.) an' I **think** (*Beat*.) like, the sy**cart**rist said – there was a statement (*Beat*.) 'If – this man – is not caught, ee will murder again.'

TERRY. Yur.

JUNE. An' that if he couldn't find a prostitute – then that would **could** be – a just an ordinary – woman. (*Beat*.) So that – made people a little bit / (*Beat*.) scary.

TERRY. / That made, uh – **that** made the area (*Beat*.) more, uh – vulnerable in that sense.

Section Three

London Road sitting rooms.

DODGE. The first girl went missing an' of course like erm ya know like the body wasn't found. The second girl went missing – (*Clicks fingers*.) there you go. Here come the police. Anthen from **then** on we had a police presence, around the area. Ya know from, from, from the sort'of second girl goin' missin'.

RON. I've never seen so many coppers. All from, all over the place. Somebody said there were five hundred policemen **on** this inquiry.

JULIE. They would knock on the door an' we'd have **these** forms to fill in. 'Do you recognise **these** ones?' or 'When did you last see **her**?' an' it's 'Can you remember what she was **wearin'**?'

JAN. Uh for each girls, there was an' a **team** (*Beat*.) a-a different **team** –

TIM. Yeah.

JAN. An' they **all** questioned us. (*Beat*.) I-it – it was – it / was getting (*Beat*.) awful –

TIM. / It just went (*Beat*.) it just went on and on and on.

JAN. We were **so** getting fed up wi' just bein' – asked (*Beat.*) ye know… / (*Pause.*) They were asking if you – had **nose hair** – **ear** hair (*Beat.*) ah w – ah (*Beat.*) **good**ness knows why / they – wanted to know **that**.

TIM. / Y –

TIM. / Y'know like –

JUNE. Well I fought ee was gonna be arrested.

TERRY. Err – yer mind goes blank (*Beat.*) 'Where was you on Monday night?' sortofthing – or whatever – day it was – can't 'member zactly the date – an' you couldn't 'member whether I went **out** – or (*Beat.*) an' so ya know you're think – 'W – where **was** I, what was I doin'?' (*Laughs.*)

JUNE. Then they said (*Beat.*) 'Wh – What colour is yer car?'

TERRY. Yer. (*Beat.*) I said 'Well s'outside – burgundy, nn – '

JUNE. 'What c (*Beat.*) / erm, registration?'

TERRY. / Yeah.

JUNE. Well ee dint even know that, did you, 'registration'.

They chuckle.

Men are all of them – well, if – peh lottof people are like that aren't they? (*Beat.*) **Then** he said – 'What colour eye – have you got **blue** eyes?' (*Beat.*) I said 'yes', I think –

TERRY. Yeah, you said 'yes'.

JUNE. An' ee said, 'Have you got a hairy chest?' (*Beat.*) An' I looked at him, an' I thought, you know, where is this **lead**in' to? (*Beat.*) 'An' what **make** – is your watch?'

TERRY. An' then that was – / **really** –

JUNE. / Well **then** that was really – ee said, 'I don't **know** – I don't kno' cuz he ant got that one **on** – at the time. (*Beat.*) Had you – ee dint know **which** one ee 'ad on that night, ye know? An' that was really – I thought, ee's gonna take 'im away – in a minut.

They laugh.

(*Laughing.*) An' I thought, not over my dead body!
(*Laughs.*)

Stella's Coffee Shop.

STELLA. Oh!

OLD LADY. Well we've never had anything like that before.
No. Well no I tell a lie. My mum's friend was murdered
twenty-odd years ago yeah (*Beat.*) yeah. So yeah. (*Beat.*)
Yeah she wa' murderd and they never found anybody that
erm (*Beat.*) that (*Beat.*) that **killed** 'er. Ya know so – yeah,
this is (*Beat.*) quite big isn't it? Yeah. Ha ha. (*Beat.*) We're
all a bit, ha ha – frightened to go out at night. (*Beat.*) Yeah.
But then we are anyway! Ha ha. Yeah. Yeah but yeah.

STELLA. Erm – oh I didn't put the brown sauce in did I?
Ooooh! You're distracting me! Ha hang on a sec. The funny
thing that some people say that they're terrified of going
anywhere. I don't think it's affected many people **I** know like
that.

CAROL 'CREAMS'. You have to carry on living your life. It's
a **tragic** situation but everybody has to continue to do the
good things that we do in Christian way that we do them.
Erm there's a hundred and seventeen thousand people I think
live in Ipswich. (*Beat.*) I think that's the correct figure. Ha ha
ha. We're looking for a tiny percentage. The rest of us must
stick together.

STARBUCKS GIRL 1. You automatically think it could be him.
/ That's the scary thing, you know he could be amongst us
an' loo walking around with us every day and we, we don't
know. / Which-like anyone. It could be anyone in here / for
all we know which has now really scared me / now thinking
about it. I'm just gonna like cry. Ha ha ha.

STARBUCKS GIRL 2. / Yeah.

STARBUCKS GIRL 2. / Yeah.

STARBUCKS GIRL 2. / Yeah.

STARBUCKS GIRL 2. / Ha ha ha.

STELLA. Erm, what have I gotta do next? Anybody?

STARBUCK GIRL 1. Cappuccino please.

STELLA. Takeaway?

STARBUCK GIRL 1. No.

STELLA. I might do you a coffee when this girl's gone. Ha ha
    – oh de. It's not usually quite so crazy. I think it's
    Christmas…!

Song – 'It Could Be Him'

STARBUCKS GIRL 1. *You automatically think it could be him.
    / That's the scary thing, you know he could be amongst us
    walking around with us every day and we, we don't know. /
    Like anyone. It could be anyone in here / for all we know
    which has now really scared me now thinking about it. I'm
    just gonna like cry. Ha ha ha.*

STARBUCKS GIRL 2. / *Yeah.*

STARBUCKS GIRL 2. / *Yeah.*

STARBUCKS GIRL 2. / *Yeah.*

STARBUCKS GIRL 1. *Uhm well some serial killer seems to be
    on the loose! And erm has sort of attacked prostitutes from i
    the Ipswich area. And they've bin found dead, naked, in,
    various different areas surrounding Ipswich – one ten minutes
    away from my house, which is slightly scary! An' it wason the
    body – on the land of a girl that goes to my school.*

STARBUCKS GIRL 2. *Yeah. Yeah I think cos we're in the
    countryside, you think it's safer than it actually is. I always
    cos I – lies – y'know 'Suffolk' an' everyone's like 'Oh iss
    really nice an' stuff.' Bu' then when you know there's actually
    someone out there, it's a lot more scary so I ain't been going
    anywhere on my own.*

STARBUCKS GIRL 1. *It's not safe for young girls – an' women out – / in Ipswich any more, it's not safe. It's quite scary to think how the world's come to this.*

STARBUCKS GIRL 2. / *Yeah.*

STARBUCKS GIRL 1. *You automatically think it could be him. / That's the scary thing, you know he could be amongst us walking around with us every day and we, we don't know. / Like anyone. It could be anyone in here / for all we know which has now really scared me / now thinking about it. I'm just gonna like cry. Ha ha ha.*

STARBUCKS GIRL 2. / *Yeah.*

STARBUCKS GIRL 2. / *Yeah.*

STARBUCKS GIRL 2. / *Yeah.*

STARBUCKS GIRL 2. / *Yeah.*

HECTOR. I erm, I've just go' – jus' broke up with – my – girlfriend, but – she's been living in a mobile home – on a farmyard, so that's – that's even **more** worrying. But I haven't said anything – but you do. All them things go through your mind. (*Beat.*) Jus' hope they **catch** him.

STELLA. You being served? (*Beat.*) Yes?

MARK. No.

WAYNE. We hoped it was an immigrant (*Beat.*) from nish-noff land –

GRAHAM. And if it is an immigrant there'll be uproar –

WAYNE. – and they'll send the fuckers all back.

Beat.

GRAHAM. Like I – I'm n, I'm **not** like that. I mean – I'm sure you're not **really** like that deep down.

WAYNE. **I** fucking **am**. (*Beat.*) I reckon it's one Polish bastard. (*Beat.*) We fucking **have** him.

Song – 'It Could Be Him' (continued)

STARBUCKS GIRL 1. *Something like this happens and you realise that so much –*

Fire alarm goes off.

– is (Beat.) so many things are bad in the world. That's the fire alarm we're all going to die.

STARBUCKS GIRL 1 *and* STARBUCKS GIRL 2 *laugh.*

But like / it's exciting cos nothing ever happens in Ipswich. / This is the first bit of like local scandal we've ever had. / Being girls being gossip- / mongers we're like – it's quite exciting.

STARBUCKS GIRL 2. / *Yeah.*

STARBUCKS GIRL 2. / *Yeah.*

STARBUCKS GIRL 2. / *Yeah.*

STARBUCKS GIRL 2. / *Yeah.*

STARBUCKS GIRL 2. *Yeah.*

STARBUCKS GIRL 1. *You automatically think it could be him. / That's the scary thing, you know he could be amongst us walking around with us every day and we, we don't know. / Like anyone. It could be anyone in here / for all we know which has now really scared me / now thinking about it. I'm just gonna like cry. Ha ha ha.*

STARBUCKS GIRL 2. / *Yeah*

STARBUCKS GIRL 2. / *Yeah.*

STARBUCKS GIRL 2. / *Yeah.*

STARBUCKS GIRL 2. / *Yeah.*

STELLA. It's cooking (*Beat.*) the breakfast huffer. They are coming on, they are just cooking. (*To audience.*) I'll make you a coffee now. Do you want anything to eat?

Underscored:

YOKEL. It could be ya next – next-door neighbour doin' it. Nobody did't know who it was. You women did't know who it was. So all us men, when I used to get on, when I used to get on the coorporation bus – I used to say 'I'm innocent, I'm innocent.' They didn't know. Even this bloke. I suppose – he felt the same.

GRAHAME COOPER. Yeah – we're all **guilty**. (*Pause.*) No we (*Beat.*) **no, we're not**. (*Beat.*) **No we're not.** There were **days** (*Beat.*) when I just **didn't go out** – Christmas shopping. (*Pause.*) Cos (*Beat.*) **I** suspected (*Beat.*) that all the **females** (*Pause.*) kn – **thought** – that **I** (*Beat.*) was a person who'd done this. (*Pause.*) So I walked around – with me head down (*Beat.*) didn't wanna look at people (*Beat.*) I didn't wanna see them lookin' at me.

Song 'It Could Be Him' (continued)

STARBUCKS GIRL 1. *You automatically think it could be him. / That's the scary thing, you know he could be amongst us walking around with us every day and we, we don't know. / Like anyone. It could be anyone in here / for all we know which has now really scared me / now thinking about it. I'm just gonna like cry. Ha ha ha.*

STARBUCKS GIRL 2. / *Yeah*

STARBUCKS GIRL 2. / *Yeah.*

STARBUCKS GIRL 2. / *Yeah*

STARBUCKS GIRL 2. / *Yeah*

GRAHAME COOPER. You've got this *feeling* of suspicious by *everybody* (*Beat.*) upon *everybody else*.

STARBUCKS GIRL 1. Is it him, is it him, is it him…? I don't know.

STARBUCKS GIRL 2. You did get that feeling. / You did!

STARBUCKS GIRL 1. / Yeah.

STELLA. Bye. (*Beat.*) Have a nice Christmas.

The County of Suffolk pub.

Song – 'Shaving Scratch'

MARK. *He's a white male aged between twenty-three and forty-seven. He'll live in the local area. He would have been fascinated absolutely fascinated with murders in his younger youth. He would have tortured animals up till his mid-teens as well. He's probably been married. Lives on his own but with a partner. And he'll definitely, definitely, definitely know all the victims – apart from one realistically and that'll 'ave been his one he's mucked up on because the other ones would have been absolutely fine goin' with him and it's probably why ee strangled her because she panicked.*

Beat.

GRAHAME. *Ha, ha, ha.*

WAYNE. *I'm fucking shitting myself! I'm getting mi coat.*

GRAHAME. *You work with him.*

WAYNE. *Fuck I'm leaving now.*

GRAHAME. *That is scary. Is that scary or what? I bet you're…*

*

MARK. *I uhm. I I I've studied serial killers since in my mid-teens. It doesn't mean I am one but err…*

GRAHAME. *….Ooh I don't know. Ha, ha, ha.*

MARK. *I just er, find it interesting. But as I say just to emphasise that doesn't make me a serial killer so…*

GRAHAME. *Oh that'll get you off the hook / after all that you've just said!*

MARK. / *That's alright then.*

*

MARK. *His failed relationships will be because erm he became violent when he was drunk – actually – he'll be an alcoholic or he'll have trouble with substance abuse as well.*

GRAHAME. *Mark you're describing yourself.*

MARK. *Ha, ha, ha.*

WAYNE. *What you trying to turn yourself in for. / It's not good.*

GRAHAME. / *Shall we ring the police now. It's scary.*
(*Laughs.*)

MARK. *And also in the last, last six weeks actually 'bout the
last two – two months approximately he'd have probably quit
his job or he'd be off sick or to that effect.*

GRAHAME. *Shut up now. / Shut up now.*

WAYNE. / *That's it. That's it.*

GRAHAME. *He's describing himself.*

WAYNE. *Look. I've just fucking wiped mi arse, I can't believe
that.*

*

MARK. *I uhm. I I I've studied serial killers since in my mid-
teens. It doesn't mean I am one but err…*

GRAHAME. *…Ooh I don't know. Ha, ha, ha.*

MARK. *I just er, find it interesting. But as I say just to
emphasise that doesn't make me a serial killer so…*

GRAHAME. *Oh that'll get you off the hook / after all that
you've just said!*

MARK. / *That's alright then.*

*

MARK. *He er. He'll be a local in the local pubs. He'll be a bit
of a loner. So that's – spot on who he is.*

WAYNE. *Mark! What you? (Beat.) What are you on?*

GRAHAME. *You are worrying me / because I remember a
couple of weeks ago when that first girl went missing you
come in the pub with blood pouring out your face.*

WAYNE. / *What you on?*

MARK. *No I did / not.*

WAYNE. / *You did!*

GRAHAME. *No I'm sorry you did come in the pub with blood coming out of your face.*

MARK. *Actually I did didn't I?*

GRAHAME. *You did!*

MARK. *Yeah. (Pause.) Shaving scratch.*

GRAHAME. *I have bin – I tell you what I have been thinking about it. I thought oh. / Half a million quid! Now you're worried aren't ya? (Pause.) Right we gotta go we'll leave you with him. (Laughs loudly) We'll come back next week.*

WAYNE. / *I've bin thinking about it.*

*

MARK. *I uhm. I I I've studied serial killers since in my mid-teens. It doesn't mean I am one but err…*

GRAHAME. *….Ooh I don't know. Ha, ha, ha.*

MARK. *I just er, find it interesting. But as I say just to emphasise that doesn't make me a serial killer so…*

GRAHAME. *Oh that'll get you off the hook / after all that you've just said!*

MARK. / *That's alright then.*

Section Four

London Road sitting rooms.

TIM. **I** get up at (*Beat.*) I-**I'm** up at five – 'bout five, quarter-
past five. (*Pause.*) An' I'm normally, sittin' here (*Beat.*)
eatin' a bowl a cereal (*Pause.*) an' I flick through Teletext –
to see if there'd been any developments, (*Laughing.*)
during the night, throughout the world, you know (*Beat.*)
an' I could hear these – car – doors closin'. (*Beat.*) An'
voices (*Beat.*) outside (*Beat.*) I was peekin' outta the
curtain – and the road was just full of p'licemen. (*Beat.*)
'Undreds of 'em.

JAN. He – h-**he** dint come and **tell** me w-exactly what was
going on, did you – or (*Beat.*) or – ah – and –

TIM. Thought it'd be a surprise.

Pause.

JAN. And, so I thought – put my head out the door an' said, 'Do
you want a cup of tea?' (*Beat.*) And they said 'Ooh – yes
please.' (*Beat.*) An' I looked up an' then (*Laughing. Beat.*)
all the p'licemen, loadsa p'licmen down here, an' loadsa the
p'licemen down – I thought there was **two**. (*Pause.*) An' I
thought – 'I ca… I gotta get t' work, I (*Laughing.*) can't give
'em **all** a cup a tea.' (*Breaking into a laugh.*)

Song – 'That's When it All Kicked Off'

RON. *I got up and all I could see was police cars* (*Beat.*)
goin' up the road. Course – ya know – I –
we knew obviously in charge –
ya know – somethin' to do with these poor girls.
But uhm –

ALL. *And that's when it all started – it all kicked off.*

JULIE. *Well I got woken up by the telephone.*
My son erm rung me on his mo – on my home phone.

I said 'Where are you?'
He said 'Well I'm down, I'm down the road
But you need to tell the police that I'm your son.'
I said 'Why what have you done?'

ALL. *And that's when it all started – it all kicked off.*

JUNE. *And you went to wor go te work, didn't you,*
and / you couldn't – w, course ee couldn't get froo.

TERRY. / *Yeah. (Beat.) An' I thought well (Beat.)*
– 'What is', well, you know – 'What's goin' on?' – ye'ow.

ALL. *And that's when it all started.*

JULIE. *He said 'No, no no, we're not allowed down the road'*
And lo and behold there was poli –
There was cameras – there was from the Sun.
You looked up the road an' all you saw was a
A tented, a tented area uhm outside number 79.
An' I thought, 'Oh no. There's another prostitute been
    found.'

VARIOUS. *I got up and all I could see was police cars (Beat.)*
goin' up the road. Course – ya know – I –
we knew obviously in charge –
ya know – somethin' to do with these poor girls.
But uhm – And that's when it all started – it all kicked off.

Repeat by ALL.

HELEN. *You looked out of the window didn't you?*

GORDON. *Well yeah*
    Cos there's a window up there /
    So you can see right over the next-door house
    An' sort of police all round there –
    blue tape everywhere an' everything.
    So I thought 'Oh, something's going on there.'

HELEN. / *Oh yeah on our landing –*

GORDON. *But then we –*

HELEN. *But we thought no more of it really didn't we?*

GORDON. *Well I wouldn't say we didn't – /*
we thought quite… / we thought about it all morning really.
But we went off to work, /
But then we started hearing on the news,
that someone had been arrested there –
or someone had been arrested.
We put two and two together,
'I think they've just arrested our next-door neighbour.'

HELEN. / *No.*

HELEN. / *No we thought about it a lot.*
No but we went off to ss… ss –

HELEN. / *Work yeah.*

RON. *I got up and all I could see was police cars (Beat.)*
goin' up the road. Course – ya know – I –
we knew obviously in charge –
ya know – somethin' to do with these poor girls.
But uhm –

Underscored:

By seven o'clock the press were here. They were stuck in
front gardens with cameras and God knows what.

ROSEMARY. They were / parking all over the place. It was
pretty awful.

RON. / Yeah.

RON. **And** knocking on doors. They **were** intrusive. They were
a **damn** nuisance. We had… I think four perhaps five…
knock on the door. In fact I said I was gonna put a turnstile
out there to charge 'em admission.

DODGE. There was tapes from this – house – here. S' I went
down to the er-police lady and 'Ohh, what's going on?' Said
'Oh there's a press conference at seven.' By **then**, erm
people in white suits moving around. An' looked up that way
and saw all the world's press.

Song – 'They Like a Good Moan'

ITN CAMERAMAN. *This is London Road (Beat.) so um –*
    this is, where – the second suspect, was arrested (Beat.)
    so, I fink Steven Wright, but – at's, yet to be confirmed,
    but, um (Beat.) an' it's, basicly – the p'lice got it cordoned
        off
    (Beat.) um (Beat.) they're jus' lettin' residents froo at the
        moment.
    (Beat.) So, um (Beat.) an' they're not very happy about the,
    um (Beat.) / intrusion – sortof, um (Beat.) –

JASON. / *No –*

ITN CAMERAMAN *and* JASON. *They like a good moan,*
    They like a good moan.

    Underscored:

TERRY. An, ye'ow – the biggest – the biggest problem, was –
    is getting ye car here (*Beat.*) uuuh – because there was so
    many, uh so many pa'era'ees (*Beat.*) wi' de ye'ow, wid the
    big vehicles, and the (*Beat.*) uhh an' all the discs –

JUNE. Oh, an' I told you 'bout… That was like a papperatti th'
    – house across the **road** (*Beat.*) I can show ye that (*Beat.*)
    cuz they wattid – they were knockin' the **fence** den te get in
    the garden te take photograph – cuz they were bringin' im
    out, ye see (*Beat.*) –

JAN. **I** had journalists, during the day here (*Beat.*) / knockin' on
    the door, I wouldn't speak to them. / I –

TIM. / Did you?

TIM. / It was absolute **chaos**. (*Pause.*) There was – TV vans all
    the way down the (*Laughing.*) road (*Beat, laughs.*) right the
    way downta the **Post** Office. (*Beat.*) Great big **cranes** up –
    arc-lights all over the place.

ITN CAMERAMAN. *Iss like, the sa'ellite trucks, the cherry-*
        pickers –
    they, they run from five in the mornin' –
    te ten or eleven, at night –

an' they're all on genera'ors they're runnin' all the time
      (Beat.)
and, the lights, there's bright lights, as well (Beat.)
so, um – they're not happy –

JASON. *But they all still watch the news and buy / the papers –*

ITN CAMERAMAN. / *Yeah they all – yeah, exactly, yeah.*

ITN CAMERAMAN *and* JASON. *They like a good moan,*
      They like a good moan.

   Underscored:

HELEN. So we, we came in and then the – then the phone rang.
   And my daughter said, 'I've just seen you come' – she lives
   in Manchester – 'I've just seen you come home.' I said
   'What?' She said 'Yeah.' So... So then the strange thing was
   we then, we then turned on the television sort of w...
   watching ourselves almost ya know. It was – because they
   were actually filming the house while we were sort of
   watching thinking 'Ooh we are inside there.' So it was all
   alittle bit weird. It was – it was –

GORDON. E-mails from people in Singapore saying 'I've just
   seen your house on the telly.'

HELEN. Yeaah.

ROSEMARY. Cos they live next door ya see which is ev, ya
   know, sort of even worse for them becos they were on
   television every day.

RON. I can't imagine what they went through. It must ha' bin
   awful for them.

ITN CAMERAMAN. *I'm uh – I'm workin' fer, oh ITN today*
   (Beat.) I'm – on standby, in case – somefing breaks an' I've
   gotta – rush off somewhere, at least – there's a cameraman in
   the area. (Beat.) Cuz, ovisly, the story's – unfolding all the time
   (Beat.) ann, there could be somefing else, breaking, you know.

JASON. *Me, I'm uh, uh – I'm a freelance, photographer (Beat.)*
   but I'm – working for – some a the nationals, today. (Beat.)

Uum (Beat.) an' from our point of view iss sorta run outta, s-
s-steam a bit, with things ta, photograph – but ya know it
was like (Beat.) every day – somebody else / (Beat.) was
found i-it almost became, like a daily occurrence of wh, ye
know, where we gonna go this morning, an' an', and (Beat.)
who's the next poor soul who's gonna – front up – in a field.
Cuz, ovisly, the story's – unfolding all the time (Beat.) ann,
there could be somefing else, breaking, you know –

JASON. / *It's a bit of a sortof an impasse, really, there's not,*
really – much, to, um (Beat.) much to do. And I'm just um
(Beat, laughs.) An' an' moa – moaning about rates an'
people wanning us to work on Christmas Day. The wife said
I can do it if it's a thousand pounds, and we'll go on holiday
afterwards, but (Beat.) part from that nah.

ITN CAMERAMAN. *They're runnin' all the time (Beat.)*
and, the lights, there's bright lights, as well (Beat.)
so, um – they're not happy – so –
But err –

JASON. *Cos they all still watch the news and buy / the papers –*

ITN CAMERAMAN. / *Yeah they all – yeah, exactly, yeah.*

ITN CAMERAMAN *and* JASON. *They like a good moan,*
They like a good moan.

LIDL car park at the end of London Road.

Underscored:

LIDL MAN. But err, it's getting really a bit err. I think it's
getting borin' now. In as much as (*Beat.*) there's nothing
happenin' is ther? Ya see what would really make a
difference now is if some – another girl was found murdered.
/ Whilst these two – whilst these two are in custody. Don't
you think?

LIDL WOMAN. / Which is a horrible thought isn't it? It's a
horrible thought. And then yerr, it's a **horrible thought**.

Song – 'My Opinion'

LIDL MAN. *Don't you think that's a load of old codswallop?*
This is my opinion. Cos I'm an ex-cop you see.

LIDL WOMAN. *Too many police doing nothing –*

LIDL MAN. *No that's not a comment –*

LIDL WOMAN. *What I mean is they're all wandering about –*

LIDL MAN. *If you wheel somebody into the station*
Without a sort of charge within twenty-four hours,
My opinion is they are not guilty.
The whole thing is a bit of a nonsense.

LIDL WOMAN (*simultaneous*). *Too many police doing nothing.*

LIDL MAN (*simultaneous*). *Innit really? This is my opinion.*

LIDL WOMAN. *His opinion.*

LIDL MAN. *Don't quote my name will you though.*
The first one who was arrested
They did a erm forensic test on his house in November…
Then there were subsequent murders weren't there…?
If you've had your house forensically checked
Would you really then go out and do a murder?
I wouldn't think so would you?
My opinion is they are not guilty.
The whole thing is a bit of a nonsense.

LIDL WOMAN (*simultaneous*). *Too many police doing nothing.*

LIDL MAN (*simultaneous*). *Innit really? This is my opinion.*

LIDL WOMAN. *His opinion.*

LIDL MAN. *Don't quote my name will you though.*
I was an old, I was an an old-time copper.
We went on our cycle on our own,
With just whistle, a truncheon that's all,
We didn't have all these police cars.
We just knocked on the door,
Sorted the murder out and left on our bike.

LIDL MAN *and* LIDL WOMAN. ***Ha ha ha ha ha ha.*** *Ha ha ha.*
My opinion is they are not guilty.
The whole thing is a bit of a nonsense.

LIDL WOMAN *(simultaneous)*. *Too many police doing nothing.*

LIDL MAN *(simultaneous)*. *Innit really? This is my opinion.*

LIDL WOMAN. *His opinion.*

LIDL MAN. *Don't quote my name will you though.*

LIDL WOMAN. I'm gonna wait for my bus now in case it
comes. / It was nice to speak to you which I didn't much but
there you go.

LIDL MAN. / Ha ha. Bye bye dear.

LIDL MAN. They won't come and look for me now will they?

LIDL WOMAN. Don't get too cold hanging about.

Section Five

London Road sitting rooms.

JULIE. It was a big shock. It's a totally different ball game
when he's just up the ro a few – six doors up. Ya know an'
think. Ya know – an' then-an' **then** they were saying 'Well.
Did you recognise 'im di' – but **no** one recognised him.

JAN. I look out of my window *(Beat.)* and, to the left – is
(Beat.) um, the house – that – Steve Wright's *(Beat.)* **partner**
rented *(Pause.)* um *(Beat.)* an' where he lived – and – we –
d-don't know exactly what went on – which really unnerves
me – I mean, um – my daughter-in-law – came – and *(Beat.)*
she didn't **realise**, that it was so close, bec – *(Beat.)* and she
we – 'Ahh! – My God, you're so close!' *(Beat.)* And she just
laughed, you know she thought / it was so **exciting** / *(Beat.)*
and *(Beat.)* and *(Beat.)* **I** was just *(Beat. Laughing.)* I
could've cried / *(Beat.)* **so** depressed.

TIM. / When I –

TIM. / But when I got –

TIM. / But when I got –

TIM. But when I got home that night (*Beat.*) they were –

JAN. It **was** so close.

TIM. We were inside the cordon (*Beat.*) –

JAN. But, I felt so (*Beat.*) **helpless** really, / because I – you know, I (*Beat.*) –

TIM. / When (*Beat.*) we then went ta –

JAN. I hadn't noticed –

JAN. We were so naive erm because I don't sit there staring out the window!

HELEN. The police were jus' there erm (*Pause.*) well twenty-four hours / weren't they? They just there patrolling. And any pedestrian who walked past was stopped.

GORDON. / Twenty-four hours a day for two weeks outside.

London Road police cordon.

HARRY. Can we walk up there? I only live round the corner. We live in Rendlesham Road. I bin affected really because you can't get in an' out of the area. It's a bit of a nuisance really... But erm. Cos I wanna come through there and then come to here – but it's not happenin' is it? Do ya see what I mean? They've barricaded that off as well ant they. (*To* POLICEMAN.) Can we go down that way?

Dog barks over POLICEMAN*'s first line.*

POLICEMAN. Where you going to?... Which way are you going to?

HARRY. I live in Rendlesham Road but I'm gonna – escort the young lady back round there.

POLICEMAN. I'm afraid (*Beat.*) you have to go round...

HARRY. Back round here?

POLICEMAN. Yeah... Sorry about that.

HARRY. S'alright. When's this gonna be over?

POLICEMAN. I don't know I wouldn't be able to say –

HARRY. Fridy?

POLICEMAN. I wouldn't know. I'd be guessing if I said Friday.

HARRY. Saturdy?

POLICEMAN. No, I'd be guessing at Saturday / as well.

HARRY. / Sunday?

Beat.

POLICEMAN. Noo, I'd dunno. Ha ha.

HARRY. Chris-Monday's Christmas – it can't be Mondy-hee hee.

POLICEMAN. No at'll stay until after Christmas I reckon.

HARRY. Christmas ya reckon.

POLICEMAN. Yeah I reckon.

Beat.

HARRY. Can we jus' come 'ere.

POLICEMAN. Yeah yerr alright. Yeah no-no worries / about this but.

HARRY. / Ya see it's against the law ya see. I don't know if I'm comin' or goin' round this area.

POLICEMAN. Yeah yerr alright yerr through here. You're not allowed through this bit basically.

HARRY. Have you got the bloke that done it then?

POLICEMAN. Oh I wouldn't know. They won't even tell us.

HARRY. Won't they?

POLICEMAN. They won't even tell us if they've arrested him / or not –

HARRY. / They got that wrong bloke didn't they – the Mon –

POLICEMAN. Trimley.

HARRY. The bloke – the bloke they got Monday – he's a Pats – he's a nut job. / He didn't do nothing like that.

POLICEMAN. / Yeah ha ha. You should come an' work for us!

HARRY. He didn't do it. Lunatic Monday. I mean God Almighty! Anybody / can say – he's not Hannibal Lecter or anybody is he? / He's a simpleton. / 'I know the girls, I've seen all them girls.' Mind you – flippin' half the tow – People in th' town if you were to pull them in probably went / with them girls.

POLICEMAN. / No he's n-ha ha.

   / POLICEMAN *laughs*.

POLICEMAN. / Yeah probably like that.

POLICEMAN. / Yeah ha.

HARRY. 'Cept from yours truly.

POLICEMAN. No I was gonna say I hopefully…

HARRY. **No.** Cos I wouldn't give fifty quid to a little skaggy little whore.

POLICEMAN. No. (*Beat.*) Anyway it looks like my relief's turned up so I'm going to get a cup of coffee. Can't be a bad thing. Take care anyway.

HARRY. Okay an' you.

JUNE. They got these tapes across – policewoman there – an' then – when we went out in the **car** (*Beat.*) you had to come up – **under** the tape with ye car – an' we 'ad te say '95' / (*Beat.*) comin' **out** – goin' **home** –

TERRY. / Mm-mm. (*Beat*.) Comin' **out**, goin' **home**.

JULIE. We had no post, no bin men. Erm if we had post men a postman had to be escorted by police inside the cordon. It was like that for about a week.

RON. **But** (*Beat*.) the good side I suppose at that time, we were the safest road in Ipswich – so many police. Ha ha.

DODGE. Look I've got four or five bobbies outside my house. I'm in the safest house in Britain. Ya know. The Queen isn't as well guarded as we are. While the police is around.

GORDON. I think it was policing as we'd like to see it all the time. / Bobbies standing at the corner of your house making sure that no nasty people got near you. (*Beat*.) Ha.

HELEN. / Ha ha ha.

HELEN. You'd feel like the uhm – Prime Minister wouldn't you?

GORDON. Yeah. Ha ha. The road was ever so quiet / and nobody stole our festive wreath this yea –

HELEN. / Yeah.

HELEN. Yeah.

JAN. When somebody knows you live opposite they wanna know – think you've got inside information which I – you haven't. You've just got what's in the – the journalists are saying – the police don't tell you anything do they?

TIM. They're not allowed to are they? (*Laughs*.)

JAN. Well no no. (*Pause*.) Is all I could say was 'There are police out there! There's cordons! They-they check who you are! E – you've got to stop at the cordon and be checked who you are!'

TIM. Excuse me I got to eat.

JAN. Oh it's that smelly fish. It's Tim's smelly – the fish for the jacket potato. Sorry. I hate the smell of it.

TIM. But I must say, it didn't (*Beat*.) it dint affect me a **great** deal (*Beat*.) because, uh (*Pause*.) I presume I (*Beat*.) that's because I (*Beat*.) done three tours in Northern Ireland – and, you saw all that sorta thing practly every **day**.

BBC NEWSREADER (*on London Road residents' TV sets*). If you've just joined us it's half past nine – this is *BBC News 24* live coverage of the arrival in Court of the forty-eight-year-old man who's been charged with murdering five prostitutes whose bodies were found in the Ipswich irea-area. Steven Wright will appear inside Ipswich Magistrates' Court within the next half hour. Our colleague er Chris Eakin is at the Court. An' Chris just talk us what we're expecting to happen.

Outside Ipswich Magistrates' Court.

CHRIS EAKIN *is live from outside the Magistrates' Court, surrounded by a crowd of locals who have come to watch.*

CHRIS EAKIN. This is now the moment that Steven Wright faces the charges – is formally charged with these five murders of the five women. All of this has happened quite suddenly. A very dramatic announcement last night, late last night that Steven Wright was charged with these five murders.

Song – 'A Wicked Bloody World'

Sung by people from the CROWD *waiting with* CHRIS EAKIN.

WOMAN 1. *I've been here since about half nine. I just saw 'im come along like with the police sirens an' that an' they were, ya know… None of the phototgraphers caught 'im, caught any photos of 'im or anythin' but just waitin' to get a glimpse really… I mean I just turned round I said to mi partner I said 'Right I'm off down town.' He said. 'What this early?' I said 'Yeah.' He said 'Yeah' he say 'you wanna go an' see what's goin' on.' I said 'Course I flaming do. **Too** right.'*

WOMAN 2. *I tell you if I get hold of 'im. Ho heh heh. I really...
I've never seen anything like it. Well I only came into town
an' I. As I came down on the roundabout where the black
building is I thought – I said to my brother I said 'What's
goin' on?' I said 'What's happened?' He said 'Cos the bloke'
– He said 'He's in Court this morning isn't he?' An' then
when I came up here I thought 'Oh my word. Am I gonna get
parked?' Ha ha. Cos they've taken all the spaces along here.*

*

WOMAN 2 (*simultaneous*). *Hallo.*

MAN (*simultaneous*). *Hallo ARV.*

WOMAN 2. *Hallo. Hallo.
They're closing in.
(Pause.) They're closing
in. (Pause.) They're
obviously – he's obviously /
comin' out cos they're
closing in. They're closing
in look. That's why all the
police – I could see them
stopping traffic an' that up
there an' all.*

MAN. *Here he comes. 'Ere he
comes.*

CHRIS EAKIN. I'm jus'
hearing some sirens
actually erm – and as he's
going to come from this
direction (*Beat.*) err, we'll
jus' turn our camera round
that way just so we do, we
do actually see this convoy
– when it hap. I think the
sirens that I can hear are
over there. (*To*
CAMERAMAN.) Turn
round this way.

WOMAN 1. *Oh dear.*

WOMAN 2. *Yeah. Look at this. Look at this!*

WOMAN 1. *It's 'orrible innit eh? It's a wicked bloody world.*

WOMAN 2. *I said to my husband 'I won't be long dear. I'm just
gonna go an' do a couple of bits in town.' I said 'Alright.' An'
then when I see this lot I phoned him up I said 'I won't be
home yet' I said / ha ha ha. He said 'Yer nosey. I said 'No' I
said 'Cos if I can get to 'im I will. (Pause.) I din knacker
'im.' (Pause.) But I don't, I don't even know where they're
gonna take 'im. They won't put 'im in Norwich cos he will
get **murdered** in there.*

WOMAN 1. / *Yeah I know I've got to get shoppin' an' stuff.*

MAN. *They won't put 'im in Norwich will they, because…
zimmy.*

WOMAN 2. *Well the thing is they oughta let 'im loose. / Let 'im
get –*

WOMAN 1. / *Let the peep loose on 'im.*

WOMAN 2. *Exactly. Let 'em loose.*

MAN. *Put 'im in a hou – room full of women then see what they
do to 'im.*

WOMAN 1. *That's alright if this dies down but I mean your
daught – you still gotta tell yer daughters to be weary all the
time. An' it's an awful world to live in, like not trusting
people innit?*

WOMAN 2. *But you look right an' you think well, ya know
'Have they got the right…?' Let's hope that that – this is the
right one.*

WOMAN 1. *Oh I hope so.*

WOMAN 2. *Let's just hope. I mean there's not a definite thing
yet.*

WOMAN 1. *I mean what evidence they've got we don't know.*

*

WOMAN 2 (*simultaneous*). *Hallo.*

MAN (*simultaneous*). *Hallo ARV.*

WOMAN 2. *Hallo. Hallo.* *They're closing in.* (*Pause.*) *They're closing in.* (*Pause.*) *They're obviously – he's obviously /* *comin' out cos they're closing in. They're closing in look. That's why all the police – I could see them*	CHRIS EAKIN. Police motorbikes coming up the road – not from the direction we were expecting so I imagine this is not the convoy. (*Beat.*) Oh it **might** be actually. (*Beat.*) I think it is – these are the sirens from the right.

stopping traffic an' that up
there an' all.

MAN. *Here he comes. 'Ere he*
comes.

WOMAN 1. *Oh dear.*

WOMAN 2. *Yeah. Look at this. Look at this!*

WOMAN 1. *It's 'orrible innit eh? It's a wicked bloody world.*

Beat.

WOMAN 2 (*simultaneous*). *Hallo.*

MAN (*simultaneous*). *Hallo ARV.*

WOMAN 2. *Hallo. Hallo. They're closing in. (Pause.) They're*
closing in. (Pause.) They're obviously – he's obviously /
comin' out cos they're closing in. They're closing in look.
That's why all the police – I could see them stopping traffic
an' that up there an' all.

MAN. / *Here he comes. 'Ere he comes.*

WOMAN 1. *Oh dear.*

WOMAN 2. *Yeah. Look at this. Look at this!*

WOMAN 1. *It's 'orrible innit eh? It's a wicked bloody world.*
(*Beat.*) *'Ere they come.*

Loud sirens. The police van *leaves the Court* *accompanied by a heavy* *police escort. The* CROWD *hurls abuse at* *the van… 'Get 'im outta* *here!', 'Scum!', etc.*	CHRIS EAKIN. It looks like we got Steven Wright now. (*Beat.*) An' here we have full convoy now. Steven Wright, forty-eight-year- old forklift-truck driver.

Crescendo builds of repeated final lines of chorus.

End of Act One.

ACT TWO

Section One

Outside Ipswich Crown Court.

PRODUCER 1. Oh there you are. Are you actually going on?

FEMALE REPORTER. Well –

PRODUCER 1. I thought Claire said you weren't –

FEMALE REPORTER. Oh –

PRODUCER 1. But that was when she was in there she said oh and tell her to do a rant.

FEMALE REPORTER. Oh right okay –

PRODUCER 1. They're all starting to come out now.

Song – 'The Five Counts of Murder'

MALE REPORTER 1. *In October and December of last year.*

FEMALE REPORTER (*and two other reporters*). *Well this is
    the **third time** that **Steve Wright** has ap –
    peared in Court but it's the **first time** that he's
    formally **en**tered a **plea** he arrived here at
    Ipswich Crown Court, shortly after
    nine o'clock, this morning but it wasn't until
    two o'clock this after**noon**, that he
    stood up, dressed in a
    black suit, **white shirt** and
    blue tie, and spoke,
    clearly and **con**fidently when he was
    asked **how** he would plead to **each** of the
    five counts of murder they were read out,
    in this order. Er –*

*Well this is the **third time** that **Steve Wright** has ap –*
***peared** in Court but it's the **first time** that he's*
*formally **en**tered a **plea** he arrived here at*
Ipswich Crown Court, shortly after
nine o'clock, this morning but it wasn't until
*two o'clock this after**noon**, that he*
***stood** up, dressed in a*
***black suit, white shirt** and*
***blue tie**, and spoke,*
***clear**ly and **con**fidently when he was*
*asked **how** he would plead to **each** of the*
***five counts** of **mur**der they were read out,*
in this order.

Tania Nichol,
Her body was the
***sec**ond to be found although she was the*
***first woman** to go missing.*
Gemma Adams
Her body of course was the
***first** to be found that was*
***fa-found** on the third of December.*
Anneli Alderton
*Whose body was found in **Nac**ton*
Paula Clennell, Annette Nicholls.
*Their bodies were of course found in **Lev**ington just a **few***
***hun**dred **yards** from each other we know that*
***all, wom**en, were **work**ing*
***in** the **town**, as prostitutes and all their*
bodies were found naked. To
***each one** of those counts of murder*
*Steve Wright, er **pleaded**, **not**,*
***Guilty**.*

Timothy Langdale QC and Peter Wright QC who is the
prosecuting er barrister here have been in discussions with
the Judge about **where** and **when**, this trial should be held. In
the end it was decided that if **poss**ible, it should **stay** here at
Ipswich Crown Court and it will beg**in**, on the **four**teenth of
January **two** thousand and **eight**.

PRODUCER 1. Seems okay?

FEMALE REPORTER. Yeah. Iss fine.

Westgate Social Club off London Road, Neighbourhood Watch Christmas Party.

JULIE. Pink one number seven.

ALL. Yeahhh.

JULIE. Next one – orange forty-seven.

RON. Yes.

ROSEMARY. Oohh. Yeah. Ha ha.

   Beat.

TIM. Gotta be in it to win-it.

ROSEMARY. Ha – Yeah – ha. True.

RON. We're (*Beat.*) happy the trial's started but erm – we're a
   bit (*Beat.*) worried about what sort of the reaction the
   media's / going to have.

HELEN. / We're worried about the media, yeah.

RON. Whether we're gonna get them all camped out on the
   doorsteps again.

JAN. Yeah. I jus' wish it had been in London. Jus' – ya know.
   It's bringin' it all back.

JULIE. Blue number forty-two.

   Beat.

JAN. Oooh that's me.

JULIE. We're betta now, betta now – this time – this time last
   year – it was – complete nightmare. But it's (*Beat.*) but it's
   creepy ya know it's – I hope we find out where – where he
   killed them an' I jus' – I jus' **pray** an' **hope** that those girls
   weren't killed in the flat. I really hope they weren't.

JULIE (*simultaneous*). *Pink one eight nine.*

JAN (*simultaneous*). *We were really, we're really upset.*

ALL (*except for* JULIE *and* JAN). *Ohhhhhh- / hhhh.*

JAN. / *One eight nine?*
I just wanted him – it to be all over
and to know were tho – were those prostitutes
***killed** in that house.*

VARIOUS. *He was only there for ten weeks.*
Ten weeks.
Just a chance.
*The one place in the – in the **whole world***
where he (Beat.) went to live ten weeks.
Could have bin anywhere!
*Could have been next door to **you**!*
Everybody would rather it all went away. (Beat.)
They must have sleepless nights.
I know I do.

JAN. It was awful. I was very upset. In the evening ya know I
jus' – it was winter like now, so I jus' closed the curtains and
uhm… It really made me very depressed and very low. I just
feel it's like, / it's like a dream still. I – I don't know, I don't
think I've really come to / (*Beat.*) to accept it. (*Beat.*) I
(*Pause*) try to (*Beat.*) jusss… (*Beat.*) keep going.

TIM. / I think there's a –

TIM. / I think…

JULIE. Right we got a blue one, two hundred and one.

Beat.

HELEN. Oh yes!

ALL. Wha-heyyyy!

ROSEMARY. You do get the odd uhm sightseer coming up.
They come up in cars an' they stop an' take a photograph /
which is (*Beat.*) really sick.

RON. / Yeah.

TIM. You – / you can actually see them.

JAN. / Nobody walks – nobody walks down that road – with – with (an' I'm the same) without staring at that house

TIM. Even **now**. People **still** do it.

JAN. During the day I had quite a bit of trouble with children here, erm jusss (*Beat.*) coming an' really looking. Sss – one of them threatened me... talking about erm, 'He's a murderer' an' everything, 'You should move an.'

JULIE. / *Pink one eight nine.*

JAN. / *We were really, we're really upset.*

ALL (*except for* JULIE *and* JAN). *Ohhhhhh- / hhhh.*

JAN. / *One eight nine?*
I just wanted him – it to be all over
and to know were tho – were those prostitutes
***killed** in that house.*

VARIOUS. *He was only there for ten weeks.*
Ten weeks.
Just a chance.
*The one place in the – in the **whole world***
where he (Beat.) went to live ten weeks.
Could have bin anywhere!
*Could have been next door to **you**!*
Everybody would rather it all went away. (Beat.)
They must have sleepless nights.
I know I do.

TERRY. Oh it **has** actually – scared er (*Beat.*) er – er, a lotta the – ye'ow, neighbourhood (*Beat.*) ye'ow, **permanently** – is – uh – it's a blot on the landscape, sortathing.

JUNE. I mean Mary won't even come down now will / she walk? (*Beat.*) My daughter. Sh' said 'I'm not walking up there.'

TERRY. / Nerr.

HELEN. When they boarded the house up, that's when I really didn't like it. We're actually – we're thinking about moving weren't we? I jus' –

GORDON. Well you were.

HELEN. – Well I was because it-it. It just sort of dep-depressed me. It depressed me living next door – ya know an' I just sort of thought 'Ohh I wanna be in a nice area.'

ALFIE. I was thinking about moving once. I was yeah.

JAN. I'm moving fourteenth of March.

JULIE. / *Pink one eight nine.*

JAN. / *We were really, we're really upset.*

ALL (*except for* JULIE *and* JAN). *Ohhhhhh- / hhhh.*

JAN. / *One eight nine?*
    I just wanted him – it to be all over
    and to know were tho – were those prostitutes
    ***killed** in that house.*

ALL. *He was only there for ten weeks.*
    Ten weeks.
    Just a chance.
    *The one place in the – in the **whole world***
    where he (Beat.) went to live ten weeks.
    Could have bin anywhere!
    *Could have been next door to **you**!*
    Everybody would rather it all went away. (Beat.)
    They must have sleepless nights.
    I know I do.

Section Two

London Road sitting rooms.

Bailey the dog is yapping.

JULIE. Oi! Eamon, will you come an' control this dog. How
     many times can they fil – film number 79. They're here
     every day. Waitin' to film (*Beat.*) ya know – film for the
     news. This sint fair on all the residents – it really isn't.
     There's no one here – there's blacked-out windows 'n' doors.
     You can't – we've got – we've got uhm (*Beat.*) Jan an' Tim
     that live opposite erm who's on our committee of the
     Neighbourhood Watch. An' I think they're getting very upset
     about it all.

TIM. You said they just used the same van, all the time, didn't
     they.

     Beat.

JAN. Pardon?

TIM. They – used the same – tellyvision van (*Beat.*) the /
     crews –

JAN. / No.

TIM. Didn't they?

JAN. No.

TIM. I thought / that's what you said.

JAN. / No – no.

NEWSREADER. Good evening and welcome to the six o'clock
     / news. It was one of the world's most advanced aircraft…

JULIE. / No we don't wanna hear about the silly plane crash.
     No one died in that! Ha ha ha. I think he's guilty but I don't
     think there's stiff evidence against him. There's – it not a
     clear – it's not a clear-cut case at all.

Outside No. 79 London Road.

SIMON NEWTON *and* SEB *(his cameraman) are filming. Action moves between outside No. 79 London Road and inside London Road residents' sitting rooms, where they are watching* Anglia News.

Song – 'Cellular Material'

SIMON NEWTON. *Impossible to report because I can't use, I use the word semen. / I can't use the word semen at lunchtime and I can't use it at six o'clock. I can use it at ten a'clock but I can't use it before teatime. So how the hell –*

SEB. / *Can you not?*

SEB. *So what do you use instead? (Beat.) Love juice?*

SIMON NEWTON. *I don't know really what to say… Bodily fluids. (To audience.) Well it's just taste reasons we can't basically have a what – what our editors call a 'Mummy what's semen?' moment. Erm in the trade. Male bodily flu – male body fluid. Sounds as if he was going round spreading it all over Ipswich.*

SEB. *Boy juice.*

SIMON NEWTON. *Ready? Three, two one. (To camera.) Using his hands to demonstrate Peter Wright explained how forensic scientists had extracted Steve Wright's DNA from other ce –*

Beat.

Ready? Using his hands to demonstrate Peter Wright explained how forensic scientists had extracted Steve Wright's DNA from other ce – ce (Beat.) cellular material found in the… (To audience.) I told you didn't I?

*

HELEN. *I think he probably did do it.*

GORDON. *He must have done it really.*

JUNE. *I think he did. Definitely did.*

DODGE. *I think he'll be found guilty.*

RON. *I think he did but he's gonna get away with it.*

ROSEMARY. *It's only circumstantial evidence.*

TIM. *I couldn't sit there an' say 'Yes he dunnit'.*

JAN. **Really?**

JULIE. *He's gonna get away with it.*

*

SEB. *Still running.*

SIMON NEWTON (*to camera*). *Using his hands to demonstrate Peter Wright explained how forensic scientists had extracted Pe –* **Steve Wright!** *Steve Wright – Peter Wright.*

Beat.

SEB. *Whenever you're ready, / it's running up. Okay.*

SIMON NEWTON. / *Okay.*

SIMON NEWTON (*to camera*). *Using his hands to demonstrate Peter Wright explained how forensic scientists had extracted Peter Wright's – Peter Wright – Steve Wright. This is the problem with this bloody trial!*

SEB. *Too many Wrights.*

*

HELEN. *I think he probably did do it.*

GORDON. *He must have done it really.*

JUNE. *I think he did. Definitely did.*

DODGE. *I think he'll be found guilty.*

RON. *I think he did but he's gonna get away with it.*

ROSEMARY. *It's only circumstantial evidence.*

TIM. *I couldn't sit there an' say 'Yes he dunnit'.*

JAN. **Really?**

JULIE. *He's gonna get away with it.*

*

SIMON NEWTON. *Ready. Three two one. (To camera.) Using his hands to demonstrate Peter Wright explained how forensic scientists had extracted **Steve** Wright's DNA from other DNA material found on both gloves. Cellular material not DNA material. This is just, / this is so complicated. How many takes did we say we were gonna do this one?*

SEB. / *Still running.*

SEB. *I don't know.*

Beat.

SIMON NEWTON. *Okay.*

SEB. *Right it's running up. Okay.*

SIMON NEWTON (*to camera*). *Using his hands to demonstrate **Peter** Wright explained how forensic scientists had extracted **Steve** Wright's DNA from other cellular material inside the thumbs of both gloves. Doctor Hau said that within that he'd f – within that cellular material.*

Beat.

SEB. *It's runnin' up.*

SIMON NEWTON. *Shall we just say sperm? (Beat.) Sorry.*

*

HELEN. *I think he probably did do it.*

GORDON. *He must have done it really.*

JUNE. *I think he did. Definitely did.*

DODGE. *I think he'll be found guilty.*

RON. *I think he did but he's gonna get away with it.*

ROSEMARY. *It's only circumstantial evidence.*

TIM. *I couldn't sit there an' say 'Yes he dunnit'.*

JAN. **Really?**

JULIE. *He's gonna get away with it.*

DODGE. *I think – I think he'll be found guilty but like the thing that for me erm is circumstantial. But I mean it was te blood on 'is jacket – two spots of blood. If he's found not guilty I mean all – all that's been done is that it hasn't **proved** is all isn't it? He isn't (Beat.) not guilty if you know what I mean? Call me kangeroo jur – the kangaroo-court advocate but I mean to me. It's jus' too much – it's too much evidence. An' if he's like ya know, seems to believe that was all a coincidence – a hell of a coincidence. Two would be a coincidence. Three is a – four – five – is jus' pushing the realms of coincidences isn't it, I think?*

ALL. *Two would be a coincidence. Three is a – four – five – is jus' pushing the realms of coincidences isn't it, I think?*

Bailey the dog barks.

JULIE. Isn't anyone there. It's probably the film crew. Bailey get down.

ANGLIA NEWSREADER (*on TV*). Steve Wright denies killing five women who worked as prostitutes in Ipswich in late 2006. With the latest from the days proceedings here's Simon Newton.

SIMON NEWTON (*on TV*). For a second day DNA expert doctor Peter Hau from the forensic science service arrived at Ipswich Crown Court in a van. Today the jury heard more about this pair of gardening gloves. They were found inside a high-vis jacket recovered from Steve Wright's house at 79 London Road.

JUNE. Ooh the house. (*Beat.*) It's here. (*Pointing up the road.*)

SIMON NEWTON. *Using his hands to demonstrate **Peter** Wright explained how forensic scientists had extracted **Steve** Wright's DNA from other cellular material inside the thumbs of both* *gloves. Doctor Hau said that within that cellular material he'd found the incomplete profile matching the fifth victim. The chance of it not being hers 'one in a billion' he said.*

ALL. *Using his hands to demonstrate* **Peter** *Wright explained how forensic scientists had extracted* **Steve** *Wright's DNA from other cellular material inside the thumbs of both gloves. Doctor Hau said that within that cellular material he'd found the incomplete profile matching the fifth victim. The chance of it not being hers 'one in a billion' he said.*

ANGLIA NEWSREADER (*on TV*). *Simon thank you.*

JULIE. Shoosh. That's gotta be **him** then.

SEB. That's the one.

SIMON NEWTON. Seriously?

SEB. That's fine that made sense. That make sense to you? Yeah. (*Beat.*) Yeah. That's alright. That all works. We got it.

London Road sitting rooms.

RON. We don't **see** the prostitutes any more.

ROSEMARY. No. They've cleaned up the area.

RON. The police have assured us (*Beat.*) that uhm (*Beat.*) they're gonna keep this up – I think that's –

ROSEMARY. Cos that-cos that's the main idea. They're tryin' to get them off the drugs. Cos that's the problem.

RON. They're tryin' to do that but **our** main job at the moment is to keep (*Pause.*) ah – ah k – we kee – w – w – keep 'em keep ah our priorities / (*Beat.*) **straight**.

ROSEMARY. / Yeah. Yeah.

RON. The people oo live ere just becau – just as entitled – to (*Beat.*) all the good things in life as the prostitutes are – / they do **all sorts** of things for these girls, s – s – they all – even offer 'em free dentistry now (*Beat.*) yet the ordinary (*Beat.*) run-of-the- / (*Beat.*) mill people – person 'as –

ROSEMARY. / Mm.

ROSEMARY. / Mm.

RON. – job findin' a dentist.

ROSEMARY. Yeah.

> *Beat.*

RON. **Before** (*Beat*.) these murders (*Beat*.) the police didn't do anything (*Beat*.) / round 'ere.

ROSEMARY. / It was a tolerance zone really.

RON. Yeah. / Yeah.

ROSEMARY. / Yeah.

HELEN. – D'ya see the police (*Beat*.) **have** (*Beat*.) ignored the problem (*Pause*.) / really (*Beat*.) –

GORDON. / Mm – they have.

HELEN. – I mean – the they –

GORDON. They would deny it, but –

HELEN. They **will** deny it but they have **ignored** they – **ignored** the problem of the prostitutes.

GORDON. Mm.

JAN. It was sort of six years ago **when** Portman Road started expanding their football team an' a new ss – err a new stadium went up that (*Beat*.) the prostitutes seemed to **come** up this way. We had reported prostitutes – I confronted one. I said 'Get out of my road. I'll call the police!' She said 'Call the police!' and I did. / Ha ha ha. Ha ha. They're so so sort of hard – **hardnosed** aren't they?

TIM. / Well, I, I informed – once they'd all been found an' they – they… they…

DODGE. We'd a **girl** at the bottom of me **drive**, she was actually leaningin the car, I said – ja-says 'D'ye mind, sortof moving off' I said, 'jus' ' – I swore at her (*Beat, laughs*.) I I admit (*Beat*.) anyway, she sayin' like, 'If you keep on at me, I'm gonna – g – I'll sort of **get** my people ta come an' burn your house down.' (*Beat*.) I 'mediately reported 'at ta the p'lice but never got anythin' – they never came – an' interviewed me (*Beat*.) –

JULIE. I don't want girls (*Beat*.) erm doin' what they did on the streets and they weren't jus' (*Beat*.) getting in people's cars they were (*Beat*.) doin' it down the alleyways an' everything else. I don't want my children to see that. Ya know the worse thing is it brings (*Beat*.) it brings the guys that want the girls. Ya know an' that's the – that's the danger of it. I I was makin' phone call after phone call each night at one stage. (*Beat*.) There was just no getting rid of them an' the only time that we got rid of them is (*Pause*.) becos they're not 'ere any more.

RON. Yeah an' the **police** – really **did** get a s – a smacked wrist. It's taken five murders to (*Beat*.) make 'em pull their finger out.

ROSEMARY. Concentrate their minds.

JUNE. We saw the odd one or two.

TERRY. I-I got approached a couple of times an' said 'Ohh, are you ya know looking for business?' an' 'No thank you darling' ya know an' 'Goodnight' –

JUNE. I did say one night to you didn't I 'She might not ever come back.'

Pause.

TERRY. No it was a big shock to the – to the neighborhood an –

JUNE. I don't think anybody really thought that they were bad girls. Ya know, I mean they **were** in a way but (*Beat*.) they weren't hurtin' anybody else were they? That was only theirselves that they were d – hurting weren't it?

TERRY. But it's like-like the other girl what we use to see up the caff isn't-it?

JUNE. Yeah. What's happened to her?

TERRY. Well we don't know what's happened to her. Very er very err petite / girl.

JUNE. / Lovely-lookin' girl – / a which-which a lot of them are int they?

TERRY. / Lovely –

Iceni Project Rehab Centre, Ipswich.

REBECCA. Yeah. No really the old bill didn't really bovver us an' that's the truth. / It was no big, no big deal at all really. Now an' again they'd stop us and I that that was just because their bosses had told them that they / oughta do something about it.

NICOLA. / No.

SARAH. / That they had to.

REBECCA. Cos I mean there was a lot of us out at one time.

SARAH. Yeah there was. At one point –

REBECCA. There must ha' bin thirty gels out there.

SARAH. Yeah. Not just sort of like – between –

REBECCA. These are not from just Ipswich – Colchester, Chelmsford.

NICOLA. All over the place.

Very long pause.

Song – 'We've All Stopped'

REBECCA. *We've all / stopped.*

SARAH. */ We've all stopped / workin' now.*

NICOLA. */ We've all stopped now. An' it – an' it has been because of the murders that we've all stopped.*

SARAH. *An' it / has yeah. That's why like we all stopped. I stopped like a month before the murders.*

SARAH. / *I've got well. Sayin' that – I got regulars / that phone and we see, ya know. We won't work the street but got a few regulars that keep us goin'.*

REBECCA. / *We got regulars yeah.*

SARAH. *Even since the murders took place like there's no point goin' down there for one becos / all the cars get stopped and you just get arrested all the time.*

NICOLA. / *Just getting arrested all the time. Gettin' stopped. They weren't like nickin' us they were like nickin' the men.*

SARAH. *They jus' stopping all of the men.*

NICOLA. *I wanna get myself clean if I can do anything ya know like I get myself clean for them almost / do ya know what I mean? Yeah cos it's like. Ya know's there's – cos the help – there's –*

SARAH. / *That what – that's what I've done. That's what I've done. Got like – getting myself clean out of – since the murders.*

NICOLA. *There's been help given us yeah. There's girls that ent took it / an' the girls – the girls that have took it –*

SARAH. / *An' we've took it.*

NICOLA. *– an' the girls that have took it a lot of them are doin' really well / an' ya know it's been a year later now –*

SARAH. / *I come 'ere four times a week.*

NICOLA. *– an' yeah, I come 'ere about three (Beat.) times and – with other organisations an' stuff. Ya know there has been the help there ya know.*

SARAH. *An' jus' do like instead of hundreds pounds' worth of drugs a day now all I do is like fifteen pounds' worth of drugs a day now if that / but if I get the money…*

NICOLA. / *I don't use every day any more. Maybe occasionally now I still use. I'm still tryin' to get over that hurdle but from where / from where I am now to what I was a year ago like there is such a change. I never thought I'd get back to where I am now I really didn't.*

SARAH. / *It's jus' that last little bit gotta get off. Yeah. I didn't think I'd ever get down to what I have. Like I've never been this big either I was like a size fucking six –*

NICOLA. *I know put on weight.*

REBECCA. *We've all put on weight! Yeah. It took all that for anyone to start helpin' us.*

SARAH. *Yeah that's what upsettin'. It took those – it took five girls. That's what make me feel I wanna get clean for 'em because it's took their lives for them to think about and go 'Come on. Let's get these girls off the street.'*

SARAH. *It took their lives for them to help us.*

Section Three

London Road sitting rooms.

ANGLIA NEWSREADER (*on TV*). *Anglia Tonight*'s Simon Newton has been following events in Court today. Simon –

SIMON NEWTON (*on TV*). Well we expect the Judge to conclude his summing up tomorrow lunchtime and we expect the jury to retire to consider its verdict some time tomorrow afternoon.

JUNE. Ohh. Well – tomorrow afternoon. You better be here tomorrow afternoon.

Courthouse Café.

KELLY McCORMACK. Now it's the waiting game. You – we're all waiting together.

A tannoy sounds.

SIMON NEWTON. They're doing this now just to tease us all –

TANNOY. All parties – in the case of Ronnie Tretton Court Four...

SIMON NEWTON. It's the phoney war – sort of stage – everyone's just s – sitting around waiting for it to um – happen. Everyone's li – gasping over their – gazing over their laptops at each other, to check whether anyone else has got something you haven't – and (*Beat.*) then it's all gonna go ballistic (*Beat.*) at some point…

TANNOY. All parties – in the case of David Hughes –

KELLY McCORMACK. Er… (*Beat.*) But it – there's that **momentary pause** every time that goes off – it's awful. We're all (*Beat.*) very **family-oriented** now, and everyone's looking after each other and buying each other coffee – as soon as that verdict's in it's gonna be an absolute – **mmmayhem**… It's dog-eat-dog as **soon** as that verdict comes out – **guaranteed**. I can promise you that.

Everyone quickly starts leaving the café.

KELLY McCORMACK. *What's happening?*

SIMON NEWTON. *Dunno. Okay. See ya later. It's one of those ju –*

KELLY McCORMACK. *Is it a jury question?*

SIMON NEWTON. *I don't know. Peter Wright's just walked down and gone (Beat.) like that to them. So everyone's going.*

KELLY McCORMACK (*excitement*). *Oh!*

SIMON NEWTON. *Because that's what we do.*

The sound of laptops being packed away, chairs being moved as the media pack leaves the room in a frenzy.

Outside the Courthouse.

PRODUCER 2. *Hi. This could be the verdict. Could be the verdict. (Pause.) Could be the verdict.*

MALE REPORTER 2 (*on his mobile*). *Hallo Victoria.*

Pause.

> *They think it might be a verdict (Beat.) and the digilink's*
> *gone down – I told the desk. (Pause.)*
> *Okay – good luck – bye… Broke!*

PRODUCER 2. *Can you do the levels again please Cole? Can*
you do the level please.

FEMALE REPORTER. *Yeah well the jury of nine men and*
three women started – deliberating –

PRODUCER 2. *You – excuse me. Can you not… Can you just*
not. Keep away. Sorry.

CAMERAMAN. *We're not on the satellite.*

MALE REPORTER 2. *Hey?*

CAMERAMAN. *We're not on the satellite!*

MALE REPORTER 2. *What day is it, Thursday? (Beat.) They*
went out Tuesday – didn't they?

Song – 'The Verdict'

MALE REPORTER 2 (*to camera*). *It was – it stretched out over that – uh – remarkable six-and-a-half weeks back in 2006 – and over ten days. Now, it see – it – he did say that he had sex with four – of those women… Now we hear it's guilty on count one – that's Tania Nicol. He has been found guilty – of killing – Tania Nicol, Tania was the – first to go missing, that was October the thirtieth – or maybe even the early hours of the thirty-first – he was caught on a – an*

FEMALE REPORTER (*off-camera to the studio*). Can you come to me? Can you come?

automatic number-plate-recognition camera, he's also guilty – of killing Gemma Adams, so that's two guilty verdicts so far. There are five counts, of course, so at the moment we know that he's – guilty of the murder of Tania Nicol – he's – guilty on count three, as well – that's guilty of killing Anneli Alderton. So that's three guilty – verdicts, so far. Tania Nicol, Gemma Adams, and Anneli Alderton there are two more counts to go – those of, ah – Annette Nicholls and Paula Clennell. Those two particular women – four guilty I'm told now that ah – Annette Nicholls is also been – uh – he's also guilty of killing Annette Nicholls, we only have to hear the fifth count now – and that's of, uh – Paula – Clennell. (Beat.) She was found very very close – to Annette Nicholls, in the same area perhaps only a – a hundred or so yards apart –now he's been found guilty on all – all charges. He's been found guilty – of killing Tania Nicol, guilty of killing Gemma Adams, guilty of

(To camera.) Yes, we are getting the verdict through now – uh – Steve Wright has been found guilty of the murders of Tania – Nicol – and Gemma Adams – that's the second count of murder. He is of course accused of five – counts – of murder the jury are nine men and three women. Again, he's been found guilty of the murder of Anneli Alderton. The nine men and three women for – six-and-a-half hours – deliberating this verdict. They went out – just after midday yesterday – ah – to consider their verdict – the Judge wants that they should all agree on a verdict if possible –

He's been found guilty of ma – of murder of ah – Annette Nicholls – as well – and there's one more verdict to come out now. Members of the jury will be telling the Court. Guilty – Steve Wright – has been found guilty on all five counts of – of murder. Guilty on five counts of murder. Steve Wright, a

killing Anneli Alderton –
guilty of killing – Annette
Nicholls – and guilty – of
killing – Paula Clennell.
And now we know that he –
has been found guilty on
all – five – charges.

man – a very unremarkable
man – on the surface of
things – a man who – has –
been responsible now – we
know – for one of the most
disgusting serial killings –
in British history.

KELLY McCORMACK. *We are still awaiting news – on Steve Wright's sentencing – it's thought Mr Justice Gross will pass that – first thing – tomorrow morning. This is Kelly MacCormack, outside Ipswich Crown Court, for Classic FM.*

Pause.

(*On phone.*) Okaaay (*Pause.*) Okay? (*Beat.*) Okay, bye! (*Beat.*) I'm **staying** connected I'll keep my headphones on too.

Pause.

Um (*Beat.*) it was **quick**, wasn't it? And the adrenaline. At the moment, I'm shaking. It's a bit (*Pants, makes a two-note, deflating cry.*) ahuhahuhah. That's the only thing I can say. (*Laughs, makes the cry again.*) Hahuhahuh.

London Road sitting rooms.

JUNE. Guil'y or **not** guil'y?

The TV plays opening music for Five News.

TERRY. 'Ere y'are.

FIVE NEWSREADER (*on TV*)....on *Five News*, reminder of our **top** story now – forty-nine-year-old **Steve Wright** / has been found **guilty** of –

JUNE. / Ooh.

FIVE NEWSREADER. – murdering **five** women / working as prostitutes around Ipswich (*Continues in background throughout.*)

TERRY. / Ooh – guilty then.

JUNE. Wha? Didn't say guil'y did it?

TERRY. Yeah.

JUNE. Oh – OOOOH! (*Laughing, exclaiming*.) O-oh! That's one for me.

TERRY. Yeah. Yeah.

JULIE. Bit of a surprise weren' it? (*Pause*.) I wish I was at Court now. (*Pause*.) I was just hands up to the police, really.

JUNE. They should **hang** 'im.

RON. Just havin' a celebratory – / glass of Scotch. (*Laughs*.)

Pause.

ROSEMARY. / Well (*Pause*.) that was a surprise weren' it?

RON. Oh – ya know…

FIVE NEWSREADER (*on TV*). Our correspondent James Cope – err – was given **access** to Steve Wright's **home** – at number – 79 / London Road **in** Ipswich –

ROSEMARY. / Whoa! Bloody 'ell.

FIVE NEWSREADER (*on TV*). – in **the heart** of the town's – red-light district – (*Continues in background throughout*.)

ROSEMARY. It's **not**! (*Laughs*.)

HELEN. It was it **was** a shock, to to to – to hear it so quickly – / I couldn't – I couldn't believe it.

GORDON. / Yeeeah.

HELEN (*looking out into the street*). Oh no it's gonna be floodlights through that door again and not bein' able to see. (*Pause*.) I don't see **why** they're **here.**

JAN. I'm feeling a lot better now it's – well – more or less over, isn't it? Common sense has prevailed. Ooh.

MARY NIGHTINGALE (*on TV*). I'm in Ipswich tonight as Steve Wright is / **convicted** of one of the most –

TIM. / Ooh Mary's outside.

JAN. Yeah.

TIM. Shall I go an' ask **Mary** if she wants some chilli? I'll go
and get me autograph book – I like Mary Nightingale. She's
a cracking bit a stuff. Quick Janet gimme a pen. (*Laughs
mischieviously.*)

Pause.

JAN. You can say you seen her now – in person not just on the
telly. (*Pause. Laughing.*) For what it's worth! (*Laughs.*)
Coulda done without not seeing her really. (*Beat.*) There's
some apple crumble in there Tim if you want any next.
Alright?

London Road outside.

GRAHAME COOPER. I think we've been **scarred** (*Beat.*) for
ever. (*Beat.*) **Women** will never trust **men** again (*Pause.*) and
men – will always (*Beat.*) wonder what **women** are thinkin'.
Ya know (*Beat.*) people 'ave been (*Pause.*) yeah – **affected**
by this an' – I guess they always will. (*Pause.*) Do you know
I've almost got this mental picture of when those girls got up
to Heaven (*Pause.*) that – St Peter said, 'Come in,' and they
– and they said something like (*Pause.*) 'D'you mean it's
over? (*Beat.*) d'you mean it's **finished**? D'you mean I'm –
they can't **hurt** me any more?'

Pause.

London Road sitting rooms.

GORDON. They certainly weren't (*Laughing.*) angels.
(*Laughs.*) Ya'ow (*Beat.*) lotta them talkin' about them bein' –
lovely girls an' everything an' all **our** experiences, they're
(*Beat.*) well foul-mouthed slags, really, / who'd stab you as
quick as (*Beat.*) –

HELEN. / Yeah.

GORDON. – phuh (*Beat.*) you know, / anything else wouldn't they **really**, I mean they –

HELEN. / Well (*Beat.*) ya'ow (*Beat.*) the the that might be a bit of an exaggeration, don't –

GORDON. Well – a slight exagger – / well they do – **rob** you (*Beat.*) –

HELEN. / But (*Beat.*) but they do **pester** you...

GORDON. – they'd easily **rob** you as much as / anything else.

HELEN. / Yeah.

DODGE. **Their** whole attitude – with us (*Beat.*) ff – makes it really **hard** – f-fer me to have much sympathy – **for**, you know what happened.

JULIE. I can imagine for erm people that lived outside the area where the prostitutes hadn't affected anyone, you would get a different opinion, you would get people feeling sorry for them and so forth. Erm but to actually – for people that lived round it an' the prostitutes made our lives hell. Why should we feel sorry for them? You know there's plenty of other people in the world that need to be thought about other than, (*Beat.*) other than the girls. (*Beat.*) Ya know, I feel sorry for the families but not them. Ya know it was just a pain in the arse. They were a complete pain in the neck. Ya know – they (*Beat.*) they're betta off ten foot under. (*Beat.*) That's a horrible thing to say isn't it? But. What's happened's happened but I'm not sad. (*Beat.*) Ya know. (*Beat.*) I'd still shake his hand. I'd love to just shake his hand an' say 'Thank you very much for getting rid of them.' (*Beat.*) I-I wou – I would if I – if you the – ya know – at the end of the day – if you had the courage to do it. Then uhm, I'd shake their hand if I had the courage but I wouldn't – I wouldn't do it. But – I can have that thought in my-my head to say 'Yeah thank you very much.'

Section Four

ALFIE*'s garden on London Road.*

Underscored:

WARD COUNCILLOR CAROL. Oh God! Wow! I think he's peaked today – prac – well probably about like Wednesday. Don't you think Inga?

JULIE. Still gotta get the trophy back. Ha!

WARD COUNCILLOR CAROL. Oh God! Ha ha ha.

GEMMA. You can always joke that you've got to take it back to re-present it.

JULIE. But it is – not bein' rude but it is the best house on the street. / Ha. It is. Yet again.

INGA. / Ha ha.

WARD COUNCILLOR CAROL. He's got his boat.

JULIE. Yup.

GEMMA. Huh.

WARD COUNCILLOR CAROL. This is a very tidy hedge as well / apart from the odd little –

JULIE. / Yeah. (*Beat.*) Yeah.

INGA. Elda?

WARD COUNCILLOR CAROL. Elder – or is it uhm… / I think it's a bit of uhm… forsythia.

INGA. / Is it elder?

INGA. Is it?

JULIE. Hiya.

WARD COUNCILLOR CAROL. Oh.

INGA. Ooh.

JULIE. Oh we got the whole crowd today.

WARD COUNCILLOR CAROL. Hahaha.

ALAN. Can I have a picture of you with your –

CHRIS. Good morning.

JULIE. Good mornin'.

WARD COUNCILLOR CAROL. Ooh look.

CHRIS. Hi I'm, I'm Chris Tomlinson. I do PR for 'Ipswich in Bloom'.

JULIE. Oh right.

WARD COUNCILLOR CAROL. Oh! Hi there.

CHRIS. And Alan Dench / who's taking / photos.

JULIE. / Yeah.

WARD COUNCILLOR CAROL. / Hiya.

JULIE. I'm – I'm – I'm I-m Julie / I'm on the committee for Neighbourhood Watch.

ALAN. / Hi Julie.

CHRIS. Ah I've got your name written down on the pad.

JULIE. Yes. Yeah. He done a lovely job again.

CHRIS. Absolutely. Doesn't it look nice. Where, where are the – / have they started?… **Inga!** / Good morning. How nice to see you!

WARD COUNCILLOR CAROL. / **Loads** of people have. Do ya know. This is **such** a good thing to do.

INGA. / Aieee!

INGA. Yes. Arrhh.

JULIE. Are you alright Alfie?

ALFIE. Yeah. Go-on.

JULIE. He done a lovely job in' he?

CHRIS. Inga Lockington?

ALAN. Yes of course I do. / Of course I do.Yes. You're in mufty today, I didn't recognise you.

INGA. / Yes.

INGA. Ahh ha ha ha.

ALAN. You haven't got on the gold?

INGA. No. I've let go of my gold. / Ha ha.

CHRIS. / Arrh. (*To* ALFIE.) This is Inga Lockington. / Used to be our Mayor.

WARD COUNCILLOR CAROL. / Hiya.

ALFIE. How are you there?

WARD COUNCILLOR CAROL. Very good, how are you?

ALFIE. Not too bad – not too bad.

WARD COUNCILLOR CAROL. Hello.

JEAN. Hello. / Pleased to meet ya.

WARD COUNCILLOR CAROL. / Do you live here as well or you?

ALFIE. This is Jean. That's mi wife.

WARD COUNCILLOR CAROL. Da ban nat-yeah-but – The gardener's wife. Nice to meet you.

JEAN. Nice to meet you as well.

WARD COUNCILLOR CAROL. Nice to meet youuu.

ALFIE. This is J, this is Jean.

WARD COUNCILLOR CAROL. I love these look.

JULIE. Yeah.

WARD COUNCILLOR CAROL. They're the first like erm cornflowers / aren't they that we've seen. WOW! / An' look at that. / Bless him.

JULIE. / Yeah yeah.

JULIE. / You gotta put.

JULIE. / Yeah.

INGA. Yes. It's just / the business.

JULIE. / We gotta put. I think best front garden is ten plus.

GEMMA. Mmmm.

WARD COUNCILLOR CAROL. Best fron – What do you think?

GEMMA. Mmmm.

INGA. Yes.

JULIE. I just think he's put in a / lot of effort.

WARD COUNCILLOR CAROL. / It's soo.

INGA. Yes.

WARD COUNCILLOR CAROL. Yeah. An' look.

JULIE. It's-it's the o – it's the / o – overall.

WARD COUNCILLOR CAROL. / Par – it's nautical, / religious.

JULIE *and* INGA. / Mmmm.

JULIE. Yeah. It's got –

WARD COUNCILLOR CAROL. Floral.

JULIE. Yeah.

WARD COUNCILLOR CAROL. All of human life is here. Haha.

JULIE. Yeah, yeah.

GEMMA. Animals on the top – / **on** the window.

WARD COUNCILLOR CAROL. / Oh look! Little birds. Little seat. Let's have a little go.

JULIE. Yeah.

INGA. Oh no I'd weight it down.

WARD COUNCILLOR CAROL. Lovely. Yeah. / Fantastic.

GEMMA. / You've got – you've / got dogs over the window.

WARD COUNCILLOR CAROL. / Where? (*Beat*.) Oh. Oh
God! I love it.

GEMMA. Ha ha.

WARD COUNCILLOR CAROL. Oh oohh! Aahhh. It is
fabulous. It's jus' – look. Gnomes! Yeah. It's sort of – it's all.
The overall effect / is stunning. / Isn't it?

JULIE. / Yeah. Yeah.

JULIE. / I think – I think it's the best – it's the best front garden.

WARD COUNCILLOR CAROL. Sorry.

JULIE. It is the best.

WARD COUNCILLOR CAROL. It's a bit of Lourdes in
London Road. / Ha ha ha.

JULIE. / Knock spots of off last year's!

ALFIE *and* JEAN *laugh*.

ALAN (*referring to his photos*). I don't know where they're
going yet but erm – there we are.

WARD COUNCILLOR CAROL. I gotta say it's Jesus that does
it for me 'ere.

GEMMA. Ha ha.

JEAN. The thing is –	ALFIE. I can't – I can't leave 'em out ya see
The thing is I'll…	cos they'll –
	WARD COUNCILLOR CAROL. Oh you / have to take 'em in?
This woman (*Beat*.) –	JULIE. / They'll go walkabouts.

Excuse me!   ALFIE. I gotta take 'em in
                                       night-time.

                                    JULIE (*simultaneous*).
                                       They'll go walkabouts.

Without Jesus you   ALAN (*simultaneous*). They
wouldn't have any of this.   go walkies do they?

                                    ALFIE. Yeah. Yeah.

JULIE. No. No.

   Beat.

JEAN. He provided all of this –

JULIE. Yerr. They done – / it's bin really lovely. It really is
   lovely.

JEAN. / – the Lord.

Outside garden of No. 79 London Road.

WARD COUNCILLOR CAROL. I think we ought to note that
   the Steve Wright house you would never know – an' it's got
   gorgeous little / rows in the garden.

JULIE. / I don't – I don't wanna mention 79 at all. / No I don't
   want –

WARD COUNCILLOR CAROL. / You don't / want 'em in it?

JULIE. / Oh no I want them in it / but we do – we do it as a – as
   a hou – as a – as a row. / We do it as a group.

WARD COUNCILLOR CAROL. / Most improved.

WARD COUNCILLOR CAROL. / Ohhhh.

WARD COUNCILLOR CAROL. It's been a problem though
   hasn't it? D'ya know / what I mean like? We bring it up at
   those meetings with the police, / 'When is it goin' to be
   unboarded?' And it is. / 'Hurrah.'

JULIE. / Yeah.

JULIE. / Yeah.

JULIE. / Yeah.

JULIE. Yeah. This is the 79 anonymous. (*Pause*.) As far as I'm concerned ya know – it all got – all got to normal now. Ya know back t – back to normal the way – the way it was. Ya know. We just wanna – wanna see an end – end to it and London Road getting back to being London Road instead of being known for someone where – where the murderer lived.

DODGE*'s back garden on London Road.*

The Git Band, GORDON *on lead guitar, can be heard playing 'Rockin' All Over the World' by Status Quo.*

TIM. People sayin' that the house should ha' bin demolished (*Beat*.) but I think that's takin' it to a bit – bit too far. So I think that's good that someone is livin' **in** the place.

JAN. It would be nice if she came to our quiz nights and joined in – the **neighbour**hood really but erm er – you can't **push** people in can you so…?

JULIE. Hallo Alecky. You know where everything is don't you? (*Beat*.) First – first lots of burgers are all out – an' sausages. There's jus' – just further down there's a table with cups an' things on. An' you can put yerr – you can put yerr drink. There's a big bucket – ice bucket. So you can put yerr drink an' that all in there. An' jus' help yerself to everything. An' then it's table an' chairs all the way – all-all down – all down there for you to sit down. Alright?

GEMMA. Hallo.

JULIE. You alright?

RON. This is all part of our drive for (*Beat*.) neighbourliness / if you like.

HELEN. / Yeah to get everybody together.

RON. Yeah.

TERRY. 'At's m – 'at's m – anstead of bein' in a town. / You –

JUNE. / You don't have sugar?

TERRY. You've sort'of got **now** – a village atmosphere.

ROSEMARY. I mean we know so (*Laughing*.) many **people** now, you know.

RON. It's a terrible shame, it's – I mean, we're – reaping na benefits of (*Beat*.) what 'appened (*Beat*.) really. Which is a (*Beat*.) there's always a silver lining! Ha.

JAN. We should have been (*Beat*.) uhm – more of a community then – when all – when all – all the prostitutes were **hanging** about.

ALFIE. Everybody's doin' their gardens up now – there's no prossies on the road. All the familia-ation ya know. We get on-an'-so it's fine now. Everything's fine.

DODGE. Look. We've turned this around like. An' this is – this is – **this** is what is possible.

GORDON. It's become **so** much more than a Neighbourhood **Watch**, really it's become a real (*Beat*.) **residents'** / association-come-community (*Beat*.) pullin' together an' havin' fun together.

JAN. / Yeah. (*Beat*.) Real sense of community.

JULIE. An' we're – doin' a huge big Christmas party, hopefully – in December (*Pause*.) with a disco, and getting the community together again **there**. (*Beat*.) Yeah you're quite **welcome** to come to the uh (*Pause*.) come to our quiz night (*Pause*.) and the, uh (*Pause*.) party – that'd be (*Beat*.) be nice to see ya.

The CROWD *applauds as* CAROL *takes the mike*.

Song – 'Everyone Smile'

GORDON, CAROL *and* JULIE *all speak into a microphone set up on the stage, where the band has been playing.*

GORDON. I don't wanna pre-empt any-anything that Julie's going to say but I would like to introduce you to Julie who has **worked non-stop** to organise this event. Therefore we feel that we oughta give her the microphone now to let her make a complete fool of herself!

CROWD. *Wheyy!*

GORDON. Oh no she's making a fool of herself last apparently, (*Beat.*) so you better hang on till the end. Anyway here's Julie to (*Beat.*) give out some prizes and…

JULIE. Carol's going to do the announcing.

GORDON. And Carol's going to do some ann – oh Carol – like to introduce Carol as well then in that case.

CROWD *laughs.*

Carol is one of our local Neighbourhood Councillors, an' she was one of the judges today in the competition and (*Beat.*) well I've lost the plot of who's going to speak now so I'll get out of the way and leave it to these two.

CROWD *laughs.*

*

Applause.

CROWD. *Wheyy!*

*

WARD COUNCILLOR CAROL. *Uhm. Hi everybody. This is the second*
    Annual er traditional party in Dodge's garden,
    After er-judging the best gardens.
    And they just get better an' better every year.
    And J-Julie must just do a better an' better job every year.
    Anyway it was a real pleasure today – really good fun,

And more an' more people have made –
More an' more effort to make London Road look beauteous.

*

Applause.

CROWD. *Wheyy!*

*

WARD COUNCILLOR CAROL. *We going to do er the best*
    ***front** garden.*
    An' we've picked as the runner – the runners-up
    This – a garden where it was very difficult,
    It was a real challenge to make this front garden (Beat.)
        beautiful.
    Because basically it's all parking.
    A – it looks absolutely lovely,
    An' once you look round the cars –

ALFIE. *I'm gonna come second then.*

WARD COUNCILLOR CAROL. *Fantastic.*

    Laughter.

    TERRY *and* JUNE *come to the front.*

*

    Applause.

CROWD. *Wheyy!*

*

RON. *Well done Tel.*

ALFIE. *Well done.*

WARD COUNCILLOR CAROL. *Really really wonderful*
        effort. Well done.

GEMMA. *Look at me please. Everyone smile.*

    Repeat x 2.

WARD COUNCILLOR CAROL. *Yeah we ha – we have official photographers. We have Gemma. We're gonna have an exhibition (Beat.) an' everything.*

GEMMA. *No we're not!*

WARD COUNCILLOR CAROL. *We are, we are. Ha ha ha.*

GEMMA. *Yeah I'm next year's!*

JUNE. *Thank you.*

WARD COUNCILLOR CAROL. *Okay.*

TERRY. *Well done.*

*

WARD COUNCILLOR CAROL. *The last section is one dear to Julie's heart.*
She's the hanging-basket queen of London Road.
The runner-up er – with a garden
That we could see the improvement to from last year,
Ya know. Erm –
Inga noted the weed – the weeding that had been done.
Janet and family of 68 come to the front.

*

Applause.

CROWD. *Wheyy!*

*

CROWD MEMBER. *Well done.*

JAN. *Thank you very much.*

WARD COUNCILLOR CAROL. *You're welcome.*

JAN. *Mwaa.*

GEMMA. *Look at me please. Everyone smile.*

Repeat x 2.

*

WARD COUNCILLOR CAROL. *Now there is the absolute*
      winner.

CROWD. *Whoo.* (*Claps in anticipation.*)

WARD COUNCILLOR CAROL. *An' it is.* (*Beat.*) *For the*
      second year running
      I do believe. Alfie!

                              *

Applause.

CROWD. *Wheyy! Yeah!*

WARD COUNCILLOR CAROL. Ahh. Well done.

GEMMA. *Look at me please. Everyone smile.*
      Everyone smile.
      Everyone smile.
      Everyone smile.

                              *

JULIE. *I think this is absolutely fantastic.*
      *So many **people** here tonight.*
      *I haven't **counted** you all.*
      Seein' everybody have a great time,
      That's what it's all about.
      Gettin' together as a community.
      Neighbours havin' fun, havin' drinks together
      and really getting on with each other.

                              *

Applause.

CROWD. *Wheyy! Yeah!*

GEMMA. *Look at me please. Everyone smile.*

                              *

JULIE. *I would like to congratulate everyone*
      That's really worked hard on their gardens.
      Even the people that haven't won.

It doesn't matter –
It's sharing their gardens with everyone else
And really workin' hard
And makin' London Road what London Road is –
A fantastic road!

*

Applause.

CROWD. *Wheyy!*

GEMMA. *Look at me please. Everyone smile.*

*

GORDON. *I'd just like to point out as well.*
It does seem that God is smiling on London Road.
Cos if you'd seen the weather forecast for today.
.Well look at it now.

Repeat x 9.

Original audio recordings of various residents at the party
are heard over the PA in the auditorium. They fade out as the
music of the song begins.

Song – 'London Road in Bloom' (reprise)

JULIE. *I got nearly seventeen hangin' baskets in this back*
garden – believe it or not. Begonias, petunias an' – erm –
impatiens an' things.

ALFIE. *Marigolds, petunias. We got up there, we got busy*
Lizzies, hangin' geraniums alright – / see the hangin'
lobelias, petunias in the basket – hangin' basket. That's a
fuchsia.

DODGE. / *There's all sorts in that basket anyway.*

JAN. *Err there is a special name I just call them lilies. They're*
a lily type. There is a special name. An' for the first time this
year I've got a couple of erm – baskets.

TERRY. *Hangin' baskets, variegated ivy in there which makes a nice show. Then you've got err these sky-blue whatever they are ve – ver – ber la la. That's err little purple ones.*

HELEN. *Rhubarb, the old-fashioned margarites, the daisies.*

GORDON. *The roses have done really well this year.*

HELEN. *Gave an extra point for havin' basil on the windowsill didn't she. / Ha ha ha.*

GORDON. / *Yeah.*

The End.

Other Titles in this Series

Tom Basden
JOSEPH K
THERE IS A WAR

Stephen Beresford
THE LAST OF THE HAUSSMANS

Alecky Blythe
CRUISING
THE GIRLFRIEND EXPERIENCE

Jez Butterworth
JERUSALEM
JEZ BUTTERWORTH PLAYS: ONE
MOJO
THE NIGHT HERON
PARLOUR SONG
THE WINTERLING

Alexi Kaye Campbell
APOLOGIA
THE FAITH MACHINE
THE PRIDE

Caryl Churchill
BLUE HEART
CHURCHILL PLAYS: THREE
CHURCHILL PLAYS: FOUR
CHURCHILL: SHORTS
CLOUD NINE
A DREAM PLAY *after* Strindberg
DRUNK ENOUGH TO SAY I LOVE YOU?
FAR AWAY
HOTEL
ICECREAM
LIGHT SHINING IN BUCKINGHAMSHIRE
MAD FOREST
A NUMBER
SEVEN JEWISH CHILDREN
THE SKRIKER
THIS IS A CHAIR
THYESTES *after* Seneca
TRAPS

Chloë Moss
CHRISTMAS IS MILES AWAY
FATAL LIGHT
THE GATEKEEPER
HOW LOVE IS SPELT
THE WAY HOME
THIS WIDE NIGHT

Elaine Murphy
LITTLE GEM

Joanna Murray Smith
BOMBSHELLS
THE FEMALE OF THE SPECIES
HONOUR

Ali Taylor
COTTON WOOL
OVERSPILL

Jack Thorne
2ND MAY 1997
BUNNY
STACY & FANNY AND FAGGOT
WHEN YOU CURE ME

Enda Walsh
BEDBOUND & MISTERMAN
DELIRIUM
DISCO PIGS & SUCKING DUBLIN
ENDA WALSH PLAYS: ONE
THE NEW ELECTRIC BALLROOM
MISTERMAN
PENELOPE
THE SMALL THINGS
THE WALWORTH FARCE

Amanda Whittington
BE MY BABY
LADIES' DAY
LADIES DOWN UNDER
SATIN 'N' STEEL